P9-CLC-824

Speaking of Maine

Selections from the
Writings of Virginia Chase

Speaking of
Maine

Edited by Margaret Shea

Illustrations by Lawrence Jan Zwart

DOWN EAST BOOKS / CAMDEN, MAINE

"Not Even Solomon . . ." is reprinted by
permission of *Woman's Day* magazine.
Copyright © 1966 by CBS Publications,
the Consumer Publishing Division of CBS, Inc.

Some of the material in this book has appeared
in somewhat different form in
Down East Magazine and in *The Hartford Courant*.

Copyright © 1983 by Virginia Chase Perkins
Library of Congress Catalog Card Number 83-70935
ISBN 0-89272-170-7
Design by Lawrence Jan Zwart
Composition by Roxmont Graphics
Printed in the United States of America

5 4 3 2 1
Down East Books / Camden, Maine

To Esther and Harold Parker,
who exemplify the best of Maine

Contents

Foreword   ix

PART ONE
Sketches and Stories   1

Sanctuary   3

Grammie   12

Not Even Solomon . . .   20

A Time for Chicken   26

The Extraordinary Spring   31

Once, at Christmas   41

Cousin My   57

Black Sunday   63

Viva Victoria   71

Les Chapeaux   80

Attention: Saint Patrick   92

Do I Hear Five?   104

A House in Maine   111

PART TWO
Maine History 119

A Loyalist of the Kennebec 123
Shipwreck 135

A Maine Coast Village 153

Samuel Trask 157
Moses Davis 168
Squire Parsons 180
Mutiny 191
Village School 207
Village Library 215
Village Postmaster 224

Sources of Material
for Part Two 235

Foreword

 o one writing today about Maine can match the authentic voice of Virginia Chase. Her beguiling stories are like drawings of a master sketcher. Every line, spare and telling, reveals her distaste for flourish. Closely observed, related with humor and an affection untainted by nostalgia, the stories in the opening section of *Speaking of Maine* sound the true ring of a born storyteller.

The youngest girl in a family of eight children, Virginia Chase spent her childhood at a time early in this century when "seen but not heard" was the expected decorum. Happily, no restrictions could be placed on her powers of rapt observation nor on her remembrance of detail that so enriches these pages.

In them we read of the uproar caused by a dispute over rights to a remarkable spring; of a regally demanding Victoria who identified herself grandly with the then reigning Queen; of Grammie, respectable as a church steeple, who became an unrepentant pilferer of gardens; of Cousin

My who all too carefully planned her own funeral; of a child's growing defiance breaking loose — in church, no less — and somehow gaining not censure but, surprisingly, respect and even deference from family and villagers.

We read of her family, too: of her father, stern to the strong, compassionate to the weak, astonishingly progressive in his ideas; of her mother, competent where he was not; of some of her many sisters and brothers, a number of whom were to become widely known throughout Maine. Among these stories is a memorable one that surely belongs in the annals of Christmas classics. It concerns this family who, at a time of temporary misfortune, celebrates Christmas Eve in a cellar, coddling a treacherous furnace.

Not all of these sketches concern childhood. Miss Chase relates how, having reached the age of "woman grown," she bought a Maine farmhouse only to find it a-slither with snakes, which she determined to obliterate — and eventually did. Again, she tells how, as a young wife visiting Paris, she rashly ordered two elegant hats when she lacked the price of even one. Here in a way particularly her own she mixes humor and suspense. The last story in the opening section is written in a minor key. This is nothing less than a prose poem, its protagonist an abandoned old house standing on run-out land at the head of a cove. Despite its dilapidation, it so represents the sturdiness of generations past that it becomes a metaphor for all that stoutly endures.

Something more sobering forms the second part of this volume. Of two notably researched accounts, the first one concerns an unbending "loyalist," Jacob Bailey, who, after being ordained with London pomp as a frontier missionary, was assigned to the region of the Kennebec. Settling in what was later to become Pownalborough, he began his strenuous mission, sometimes walking as many as fifty miles at a stretch in all weather. During the Revolutionary War, he met with barbaric treatment at the hands of the new "patriots" because of his adherence to the Crown. Finally, destitute, he fled with other loyalists to Halifax.

The second account, "Shipwreck," relates the complete story, insofar as it ever will be known, of the loss of the steamer *Portland* in November 1898. In one of the worst storms that ever struck the northeast, this elegantly appointed sidewheeler went down, with up to two hundred passengers and crew members. Though the United States District Court eventually held that the disaster had occurred "by Act of God and perils of the sea," no specific reason for it could be determined. Beyond a few battered bodies and fragments of wreckage, no trace of the vessel has ever been found.

Following these two harrowing tales is an examination, if you will, of our rough Maine beginnings. Scrupulously documented, this series of historical accounts centers on the small coastal town of Edgecomb, which lies midway between Wiscasset and Boothbay Harbor. Edgecomb was a natural choice, for the writer spent ten summers there.

Not so well-known as many coastal villages, Edgecomb luckily had as early settlers a goodly share of hardy, responsible men. One was Samuel Trask who, taken captive by the Indians when he was only eight years old, was not to become a free man for fourteen years — and lived, according to some accounts, to be 118. Another was the enduring Moses Davis, diarist, coffin-maker, insatiable drinker of tea, ferryman, surveyor, lover of fine clothes. Still another was country squire and entrepreneur Stephen Parsons, the prototype of what was to become the "go-getting" American. Among the stories is the dire tale of mutiny aboard the *Jefferson Borden*, commanded by

Edgecomb's hard-driving Captain Patterson. Related in great part through the diaries kept by the captain's wife, this story speaks eloquently of the valiant women who dared the terrors of ocean passages.

What most keenly strikes the reader is the tough fiber of these Edgecomb pioneers. Lacking physical amenities, relying on primitive travel by river or over crudely laid-out roads, they survived calamitous droughts, floods, fire, and the rigors of climate with an equanimity that would daunt today's more pampered citizen. Essentially unlettered, these men yet expressed themselves tersely, judged situations with uncommon good sense, and forthrightly met every crisis.

Nor were they indifferent to educational needs. Arduous demands were made on young scholars attending the one-room school — and upon the schoolmaster as well, whose many duties included wielding a cane with deft dispatch. Ambitious, too, in the further pursuit of "culture," the villagers proudly opened a public library in 1821, its original stock of books numbering only forty. Nor did this spirit of enterprise lessen over the years. In fact, it might be said to have culminated much later in the indomitable Fanny Stone, of whirlwind energies, who served as postmaster longer than anyone in the United States: forty-seven years.

These inspiring stories, whether autobiographical or historical, bear a unique stamp, confirming Virginia Chase's place in the top rank of storytellers, in or out of Maine.

M.S.

PART ONE

Sketches and Stories

Sanctuary

here is an island twelve miles off the coast of Maine (Widow Island, maps call it) where sea birds — gulls, terns, cormorants, blue herons — protected by law, sun peacefully on the ledges and nest securely in the long, wiry grasses. Once it was another kind of sanctuary.

In 1905 my father, a trustee of the Maine State Mental Hospitals, created a sensation. Seven years before, the Congress of the United States had offered Widow Island, the site of a Marine Hospital, together with its fine modern buildings and equipment, as a gift to the state. Seeing no use for the property, the legislature had delayed action. Then, when a move to decline it had already been made, my father rose and proposed that the island be used during the summer months for the convalescent insane, where, confined only by the sea, they might benefit by sun, air, and freedom.

His proposal was greeted by a stunned silence, for insanity bore a heavy stigma then. All mental patients were kept behind bars and many of them in straightjackets. But after the shock was over, the legislators broke into protest. There would be danger, they said, and certainly violence. The public would never stand for it. Was my father crazy himself? one of them demanded.

My father was a strong man, accustomed to opposition. If patients were carefully selected, a man would be as safe on the island, he insisted, as in his own back yard. This conviction was shared by half a dozen leading doctors.

"Would *you* spend a summer there?" a heckler called.

No one had ever heckled him before. The room waited in silence for his answer. "I can't," he said. "I have a family to support. But if the place materializes, I'll send my children every year."

His confidence had its effect. The bill was passed. Six thousand dollars was appropriated for improvement and repair, and the establishment, referred to by the newspapers as "a sanitary retreat," opened in July, 1905.

A man of his word, he sent two of us children there every summer: hostages, as it were, girls with the women, boys with the men. I went first in 1907, just before my fifth birthday. My sister Olive, who was ten, went with me.

The launch, named *The Whim*, met us at North Haven, and from its bobbing deck we got our first glimpse of the island. It was perhaps half a mile long. One end was high and rocky, stained white by the sea birds; the other, low and covered with tall grasses. Here were the original buildings, all of brick. To their left was a new frame bungalow; beside it was a swimming pool and, beyond this, the wharf, where the schooner *General Knox* was docked, ready to take the patients sailing.

My sister and I had not been told why we were there or even why the women were. We saw, of course, that they had peculiarities, but these only aroused our interest and admiration.

4

At home, all grown-ups seemed alike, cut from the same pattern. It was their world, and if you were a child in it you minded your manners. You did not interrupt. You said "sir" or "ma'am" when you spoke to your elders. Before you did anything, you were supposed at least to consider what people might think or say. If your parents were particular — and most parents were — you could never go barefooted; instead, you wore long ribbed stockings which you changed every day. But on the island you did what you wanted to, even on Sunday, and no one stared. There, grown-ups had forgotten that children should be seen and not heard.

Mornings when the tide was out we tramped along the beaches, as thick with starfish as the firmament with stars. When one of the doctors or nurses could come with us, we fished from the wharf or ducked in the swimming pool where the water was warmer than in the sea. Afternoons we rested on the long verandas, where the only motion was that of our rockers and the quick fingers of Miss Gracie and Mrs. Ober, who were deaf and dumb; the only sound that of the bell buoy to the west, or the squeak of the Teddy bear Miss Susie always carried; or the gentle whisper of "Miss Longfellow" writing her poems. *Come, oh fishes, in your little red wagons . . .*

Later, if the wind was blowing, all of us — patients, doctors, nurses, children — crowded the deck of the old schooner and sailed past the lighthouse on Goose Rocks and among the little bare-topped islands. As we sailed, we sang or counted osprey or watched for seals upon the ledges. Sometimes we unbraided our hair and let the wind blow it across our faces. Sometimes we leaned over the rail and fished for flounders. Occasionally the schooner landed at North Haven or Vinalhaven so that all of us could buy ice cream or postcards at the village store. But we were never made welcome there. No one greeted us or even smiled as we walked along the streets. Instead, people stared or winked at each other surreptitiously. Children were called inside. Often doors were closed and curtains lowered. In the stores we were waited on briefly and without encouragement to linger. These things troubled me at the time, but I was a child and soon forgot.

Evenings we lighted a huge bonfire under the stars and sat in a circle around it, each holding a piece of driftwood — fagots, we called them — which in turn we cast into the fire, singing a song or reciting a poem while it was burning. The performances were always unpredictable and often exciting. We never had to sit, bored and restless, as we often did at home during a program. When a performer became tiresome, another simply got up and began an act of her own.

Where we were concerned, they were never critical. No matter how many times we repeated the same poem, we could be sure of eager, encouraging eyes.

"Bravo," Mrs. Pendexter would call, waving the open umbrella she always carried.

"Bravo! Bravo!" the others would echo.

But my most vivid memory concerns my father. Late in July of 1907, word came that he was to pay the island a visit. He was, the women had been told, their benefactor, and days ahead they began to prepare for his arrival. Every morning they swept the verandas with special care and, forgetful of the coming tides, cleared the driftwood from the shores.

"Dear Judge," they would say as they worked. "The dear Judge is coming."

Now we honored our father according to the Commandment. We admired his impressive physique; we were proud of the way people listened when he talked. But, young and careless, we saw him only as a stern taskmaster whose role, like Jehovah's, was to give out punishment.

Actually, if the truth were known, we were afraid of him, though we dreaded his ultimatums less than his long, deep silences. Thus the patients' happy anticipation made us uneasy.

On the afternoon before he was to come we were seated on the steps. It was a hot day; even the breeze brought warmth with it. "Miss Longfellow" looked up from her notebook and spoke suddenly. "I have just written a poem," she said, "to read upon the Judge's arrival."

If there was anything my father would not tolerate it was nonsense. "We can dispense with that," he would say when we started any. Besides, "Miss Longfellow" read very slowly, with intervals of silence, as though she had forgotten she was reading at all. My father had no use for slowness, either. "Come, come," he would say briskly, snapping his fingers whenever we hesitated. Then, too, we were beginning to sense that these women, though kind and loving, were not very bright. Dullness was something my father had no patience with. We wouldn't have dared to bring home a report card with less than a ninety-five on it.

"Dear Judge." Mrs. Trundy stopped — she was forever walking — and spoke out in a voice that was warm and tender. "Bless his sweet heart."

We rarely exchanged words of affection in our family, nor were such words often exchanged in families we knew.

"I shall gather blossoms," Mrs. Trundy continued, "and strew them in his path."

Mrs. Tapley, who had appeared to be sleeping, stirred. "I shall kneel before him."

My father could not abide subserviency. "Stand up straight," he was always telling us. "Look people in the eye when you talk." Yet Mrs. Tapley was going to kneel before him.

Then from the end of the veranda I heard Miss Susie's gentle voice. "I," she began dreamily, "shall kiss his hand."

Kisses were formal things in our family, exchanged only after a prolonged absence, then on the cheek, stiffly. Alarmed at what lay ahead, I seized my sister's sleeve, but she pushed me aside roughly.

That night I slept very little. I woke up tired and dressed slowly. When I finally got outside, I found that the barrels used for catching rain against a dry spell were filled with blossoms — daisies, buttercups, long strings of wild sweet pea. My sister was not in sight.

"I've picked the very last blossoms," Mrs. Pendexter said, coming toward me, holding a scrawny, wilting bunch of devil's paintbrush under her umbrella. "The next thing," she continued briskly, "is to make the wreath."

"The wreath?" I echoed fearfully.

"For his head," she answered.

I could not touch my breakfast.

At the first sound of the launch my sister appeared from behind the rocks where she had been hiding and took me by the hand. Silently we moved to the rear of the cheering crowd, watched the line thrown, saw the doctor disembark, then my father. Sick with apprehension, we saw the air fill with blossoms. Then Mrs. Pendexter advanced under her umbrella, carrying the wreath.

Unequal to what lay ahead, my sister and I, hand in hand, turned to run away. My father's voice stopped us. "Where are my girls?" we heard him say. We stood still and stared. There he was smiling broadly, the wreath circling his bald spot. "Where are my girls?" he said again.

We came forward silently, cautiously. He kissed us, not one of the formal kisses we knew, and, putting an arm around each of us, led the long, gay procession to the center of the island where a platform had been placed. When he was seated upon it, a garland about his neck and his wreath straightened, "Miss Longfellow" read her poem. He listened intently, even respectfully, seeming not to notice the silences. Then he made a speech. It was not at all like the orations for which he was well-known, but a simple, quiet speech, without even a gesture.

After the cheers, the games began. There were Ring Around a Rosie, Farmer in the Dell, In and Out the Window. My father, who never played a game with us at home beyond a brief, impatient hand of Authors, led them all: Tag, Puss in the Corner, London Bridge, which he played with Mrs. Pendexter, gallantly lowering and raising her umbrella every time they went under.

Gradually we relaxed, but it was only when the launch went out, an hour behind schedule, with him waving from the stern, that we understood, in the wordless way of children, that here, among these simple people who had forgotten all about dignity, who knew nothing about logic or argument or even justice, my father for a little while at least had been able, like them, to find a sanctuary.

We went home the next week. All during the trip we wondered, though neither phrased the question, how my father would behave when he met us at the boat. Would he say "Where are my girls" again? Would he, perhaps, put his arm around us?

He did neither. To all appearances he was quite himself. He greeted us brusquely, put our bags on the front seat of the surrey, and waited impatiently while we climbed in the back. We sat stiff and silent all the way to the village, past the stately white houses, the high prim fences, the formal gardens. We sat just as we had sat time and time before.

But there was a difference.
We weren't afraid of my father any longer.
We were never afraid of him again.

The "sanitary retreat" operated successfully for ten years, then it was given up because of the complications which war brought. Later it was used for a time as a school for lighthouse children. In 1925 the buildings were razed and the bricks piled up on the wharf for shipping.

Now only the grasses and ledges remain. Now only the birds find sanctuary there, looking from a distance like a great white cloud hung low in the sky.

Grammie

knew her only in her old age, but even then my grandmother was still handsome, with soft heavy hair, blue-green eyes that missed nothing, and a mouth that defied destiny. The years had not diminished her energy. Those who could do only one thing at a time, albeit thoroughly, she dismissed as "mere sluggards." She herself rarely did less than three.

Born in 1827 and named Eliza Ann Wescott, she was the oldest of ten children living on a farm five miles from the village of Blue Hill. At the age of three she could crochet. At five she was knitting her own stockings. To spur us on she would often relate the events of her tenth birthday when her parents, as was their weekly custom, drove into town for provisions, leaving her with the responsibilities of the household which by that time included six younger brothers and sisters.

She washed the dishes, made the beds, cleaned and trimmed seven lamps, churned ten pounds of butter, got dinner for nine (including the hired men), and then, unwilling to be idle, seized an old coat of her father's, cut, fit, and sewed it into a coat, waistcoat, and trousers for one of her brothers, completing, even pressing, it by the time her parents returned at four.

Provincial though she was, hers was no ordinary life. At fifteen she was a competent midwife, serving the entire community. At seventeen, alone, she left Blue Hill (something almost unprecedented in our area) and spent six months learning the trade of seamstress in Bangor. When she returned, her services at twenty-five cents a day were in constant demand. But the real drama of her life began only at the age of twenty when she met my grandfather, Melatiah Chase.

Four years older than she, he had gone to sea as a cabin boy at fourteen. Ten years later, as first mate on a ship manned by a Blue Hill crew, including one of his brothers, he had been the sole survivor of a wreck off the coast of Ireland. Months afterward, feared drowned with the others, he had arrived home just in time for the memorial service customary when a local ship went down. My grandmother was singing in the choir. If he had seen her before — something she never made quite clear — he saw her then with new and enraptured eyes. At that moment began the mutual and constant love that shaped their lives.

Two years later they married and set sail on a ship of which he himself was master. Undeterred by a dramatic and disastrous wreck almost as soon as the voyage had begun, my grandmother continued to sail for the greater part of eleven years, much of the time keeping her two small daughters with her. As wife of a ship's master and owner as well, she had entry to the society of many lands. She knew garden parties, dinners, balls. She also knew Chinese temples and the shops of Cadiz, Marseilles, Shanghai. When they returned to Blue Hill for good in 1861, she was a provincial no longer.

Shipping was already in decline. Having prospered, my grandfather knew better than to push his luck too far. Besides, he seems never to have loved the sea with my grandmother's romantic fervor. Glad to be settled at last, he acquired both the village grocery store and a neighboring quarry. He had already bought a house in Blue Hill, a large white one on the edge of the village, in which, on the very year of their return, my father, their only son, was born. To commemorate the occasion, my grandfather, rejoicing, had gone to the mountain and brought home (on his back, my grandmother told us repeatedly as though that in itself had a significance) elm seedlings to shade the house and grounds. All but one of those great trees live and thrive today.

More restless than he, my grandmother seems never to have completely adjusted to village life. Her social position was unchallenged. She grew handsomer with the years. Her carriage, developed on shipboard, was erect and impressive. Her abundant hair, white when I knew her and always parted severely in the middle, was kept by some secret nightly process in waves that swept gracefully into a high French twist. Her clothing, shaped, of course, by her own needle, had a cosmopolitan air. It was made not from the material in my grandfather's store, but from silks she had bought in the Orient and wools from the British Isles. In church she fluttered a fan from Spain.

Monotony irked her. Knowing that my grandfather would never willingly allow her out of his sight, every few years she schemed escape. She was, she told him, developing symptoms of cancer, then — as now — a dreaded, almost unmentionable disease, and must go at once to Boston for treatment. Agonized, he made arrangements for her to stay with the family of a minister on the outskirts of the city so that she might take her treatments in safety and respectability. Of what treatments she took, if any,

15

there is no record, for her letters home have never been found. But a number of his to her remain, touching in their anxiety and loneliness. "Stay, dear wife," he wrote. "Stay as long as you must. Do not worry. All is well here. The housekeeper is no good. The children cry for you and pray for you each night. I begin to feel poorly. Stay. Stay as long as you must."

Unmoved, she stayed until she grew restless again. Then cured, she pronounced, but only temporarily, she returned home with several trunks full of silk and calico.

At my grandfather's death in 1884, she was stunned and unbelieving. He was only sixty-one. She would neither leave their house nor stay alone in it. So my father and mother, not long married, were obliged to give up their own home and move into hers, where all eight of their children were born. "It is not easy for your grandmother having all of us here," my mother used to say magnanimously. The truth was it was never easy for anyone, for though my grandmother's heart was genuinely broken, her spirit was not.

Some part of her was always in motion. Her fingers flew, especially in crocheting, transforming durable, almost indestructible thread into lace for underwear. (There must have eventually been mile after mile of it, and hardly a child in town had not been scratched by it in one place or another.) She did not, of course, need her eyes for this. All the while they rested on the pages of some book while her foot rocked a baby in the cradle. My mother attempted tactfully to curtail this rocking, for my grandmother's reading was limited to stories of suspense, preferably violence, (including the livelier portions of the Bible), and her tempo often increased alarmingly.

No one ever got ahead of her. Few could even keep up. On Sundays, unlike other people in the village who left for church at the first note of the last bell, she was in her pew when it began, fanning herself and tapping her foot impatiently. She was already standing in the pause that preceded the anthem; and when the responsive reading began, her voice was a word or two ahead of the rest of the congregation.

Never one to help in the kitchen, she took upon herself the responsibility of getting my sister and me off to school in the morning. Though school did not begin until eight-thirty and was only a five-minute walk, by seven-fifteen she had wrenched us from our breakfast and hurried us to the back bedroom where her zest with the washcloth and comb left us enraged and temporarily exhausted.

My mother gave up early. "It is your grandmother's house," she would reply to our complaints. My father was less resigned. "Can't you wait, Mother?" he would ask, exasperated, while at exactly eight o'clock — her bedtime — she stood, fuming, behind his chair waiting for him to finish his nightly paper so that she might put it in the wicker rack above the woodbox, a self-appointed chore. "Certainly not," she answered briskly. He grumbled, but he usually gave it to her only to retrieve it when her lamp was out. Eventually, he, too, gave up completely.

Except in the winter months, which she spent in Bethel with her third and only living daughter, Mary Herrick, my grandmother made a weekly pilgrimage to my grandfather's grave. Their lot, as might have been expected, was impressive in its exhibits of granite, its entrance flanked by handsome urns intended for floral display. At first she was content with stripping our own gardens. ("It would be nice if she would leave just a few sweet peas," my mother would often say wistfully.) But as the years passed and her taste for change remained unabated, she began without reticence, much less shame, to supplement our flowers with choice blossoms or boughs from gardens on the way. As her escort, assigned to carry the pail to fill with water from the cemetery brook, I would stand mortified and helpless while hostile eyes watched from behind parlor curtains.

Since to tell on Grammie was inconceivable, it was from an irate householder, thoroughly vandalized, that my mother eventually found out. Without stopping to take off her apron, she marched straight to my father's law office. "This has got to be stopped at once," she announced. My father, mystified and shaken by such unprecedented behavior, followed her home.

When Grammie and I returned, he gave her a few minutes to rest in the parlor, where she sat in the rocker fanning herself with the Spanish fan. Then he came into the room, squared his shoulders, and began. "Mother, I hear you've been taking flowers that don't belong to us," he said.

She looked up, composed, even complacent, and answered his question with one of her own. "You believe your father doesn't deserve the best?"

That threw him a little. It wasn't quite the kind of argument he met in the courtroom. "But you're breaking the law," he protested. "Don't you . . . ."

She interrupted him but not the motion of the fan. "Who, may I ask, has the right to make laws for those who have gone on ahead?"

He never tried to oppose her again. From then on my mother spent her Saturday mornings in the kitchen, making as peace offerings cookies and doughnuts to be distributed with her apologies during my grandmother's afternoon nap. Once in a while, especially during the lilac season, a Washington pie seemed called for.

The prospect of her death was a matter of great and consuming concern to my grandmother. This concern came neither from the thought that illness might precede it nor from any uncertainty regarding her status in the after-world. It came simply from an anxiety that she might not look her best at her funeral. Following my grandfather's death she had dressed entirely in black or white (even her handkerchiefs had wide black borders), but since she had for accessories countless fichus, jabots, collars, ruchings, bolts of beaded braid, and yards of lace from Brussels, her wardrobe lacked no variety. Her problem was to keep up with the style.

In the second drawer of the spare-room bureau was a shining black satin dress which she had reserved for her burial. Each year when my sister Edith returned home for a visit, it was taken from its multiple layers of tissue and stretched with great solemnity on the parlor sofa, ready to be brought up to date. Edith was not only the best seamstress in the family, she was also, since she worked in Boston, considered, at least by my grandmother, its expert on style. "Now Edith," she would begin with rare deference, "just what are ladies wearing this year?" Season after season Edith good-humoredly tried out fichus and jabots, fringes and ruching. But one year her sense of humor got the better of her. "Grammie," she said in response to the perennial question, "I can tell you what ladies are wearing in Boston, but I cannot tell you what they are wearing in Eternity."

My grandmother lived to be eighty-six. She died, as if by her own decree, on the day following my father's death in March, 1914. At her funeral, a Presence still, she looked as though she were about to attend some function of great dignity, as perhaps she was, wearing the shining black satin with a jabot of Brussels lace which, by happy coincidence, was exactly what ladies in Boston were wear-ing that spring.

Not Even Solomon...

 have just returned from a day of shopping. Unopened on the davenport, in a gold-scrolled box, is a suit I shall wear tomorrow when I give a lecture which I very much dread. Beside it, also unopened, is a hat packed as reverently as though it were a tiara. I should be pleased, and I am. The color of the suit becomes me. The fit is good. The hat, admittedly, takes years off my age. But I cannot now, nor indeed can I ever, feel the excitement most women feel after a successful day in the stores. For in my childhood clothing that was bought — we called it "boughten" or "bran-new" — was regarded as a curiosity, necessary sometimes for an only child (both a rarity and an object of pity in our village) but somehow sterile.

Until I was sixteen and almost ready for college I had never had a dress or coat that was exclusively my own. It was not because we were poor. Compared to other families in our little Maine village we would have been considered, I suppose, well off. It was rather because we were practical. Serge didn't wear out easily nor did flannel, gingham or even faille, which we called "fillay." Waste, we were brought up to believe, was not only profligate, it was, in my grandmother's language, "downright vulgar" as well. Thus clothing was passed around as long as it had any good left in it. Then it was cut up, dyed, and made into rugs.

This was not unique with our family. It was accepted village procedure. A few children may have rebelled, but if so, they were not vocal about it. Such terms as "cast-offs" and "hand-me-downs" were unknown to us. In every case I knew, passing clothing from child to child actually enhanced family unity. For me it did more.

Theoretically I, the youngest of five girls, being plain and in no way outstanding, should have experienced deep psychological scars. But such was not the case. I admired all of my sisters. For me, Mildred exemplified the perfection of composure; Mary Ellen of imagination; Edith of competence; Olive of allure. Wearing their clothing, cut down and transformed perhaps by a new sash or a bertha, I felt, quite literally, something of their personalities carry over into mine.

Mildred's brown serge, with a double row of new brass buttons, took away my natural stage fright and enabled me to recite "The Death of Minnehaha" or "Angels of Buena Vista" with remarkable eloquence and without any urging. Mary Ellen's blue flannel, revitalized with a Buster Brown collar, drew me out and started me telling stories until I had to be stopped. A navy-blue middy blouse belonging to Edith, who had inherited it from Mildred, plus a new red tie so quickened my wits that I always wore it to school on days we had oral arithmetic. And Olive's blue and white foulard, with no changes whatever but a

21

shortened hem, made me, until then considered retiring, swish openly when I walked past the boys.

The fact that my clothing might be identified made no difference whatever to me. I can remember mounting the platform of the academy to recite "The Wreck of the Hesperus" in a white voile, thinly disguised, and hearing a low voice from the front row saying, "Looks as good on her as it did on Edith and Olive, don't it?" The words only added to my fire.

My sisters were not my only benefactors. Others were Aunt Matilda, actually a second cousin of my father by marriage, and her daughter Belle. They lived in Boston. Except for its monuments, familiar to every school child, Boston was a place we knew little about. But what we had picked up gave us the impression that people there lived a decidedly irresponsible life. They ate in restaurants when they might have cooked at home. They rode on trolley cars instead of walking. When they outgrew their clothes, they had so little ingenuity that they just went out and bought new ones.

These impressions were confirmed by the semiannual boxes sent us by Aunt Matilda and Belle, boxes whose contents, heavily perfumed, dazzled us by their variety of colors, including orange and purple, which we seldom saw outside of a sunset. They contained hobble skirts, promptly cut up for belts and suspenders; transparent blouses, which disappeared immediately; bewildering hats, obviously intended to be worn at an angle; long buttoned gloves, barely transparent veils, high-heeled pumps, and once a feather boa. Such a box meant private excitement, but little opportunity for public display, for its contents, after being hung out at night to air, were then sorted into two piles, by far the larger of which was placed in a trunk and reserved for amateur theatricals. Robert Service was our favorite source

for drama, and no other family in the village could so effectively attire "the lady who was known as Lou."

But our real benefactors were the Brighams. Just who they were I never knew, for with the acceptance of children I never asked. It is my impression now that they lived in Chicago; that their family, like ours, was large; and that they too were well off, but by quite another standard. Their coats were lined in satin, not sateen. Their dresses had belts of real leather. Their hats, cut properly, had both durability and distinction. Remade each year, the felt turned up in a new direction and secured by a buckle or a cherry, the straws retouched with Colorite, they gave us such an air that even my father was impressed. Once at Easter when the spring transformation was completed, he, an infrequent churchgoer, lowered his book long enough to look us over as we left and murmur, "Not even Solomon in all his glory was arrayed like one of these."

The only disadvantage about inherited clothing came from the fact that it had to be altered before it could be worn. Since my mother was, by her own admission, "no hand with the needle," this became largely the work of the village seamstress, Mrs. Hannah Sargent, widely respected both for her "eye" and her ability with the shears. Engaged far in advance, since her services at a dollar a day were in great demand, she would arrive promptly at eight in the morning, ready for action, a black apron tied around her solid waist, her ample bosom a handy and appropriate cushion for hundreds of pins. The dining room table would be piled high with skirts and dresses and just plain pieces, all awaiting reincarnation, and the two of them, my mother always conscious of her limitations, would begin.

The hours that followed were always painful for me. I was a small child, and since my mother and Mrs. Sargent were stout and averse to bending, they installed me, stand-

24

ing, on the table, while, taking their time, they studied the material at hand with reference to Mrs. Sargent's tissue paper patterns, almost worn out from use.

Normally inclined toward dizziness, I would stand, my feet submerged under serge and flannel, dodging the hanging lamp, while I was turned and pinned and measured. Almost at once I would yawn and sigh and slump, shifting my weight from one leg to the other, sometimes making it necessary for an entire hem to be done over. By nine o'clock Mrs. Sargent, whose own daughters were models of behavior, my mother always reminded me, would begin to show exasperation. By ten when I had paled and had to be indulged with a drink of water, she grew concerned. "I believe Virginia's going to give out early," she invariably pronounced, a prophecy I often feel has been fulfilled.

But when it was finally done, what a satisfaction! Careful not to loosen a pin or catch a basting, I could tiptoe into the parlor and behold the promise of a new creation. A high military collar transforming Mary Ellen's corduroy coat into a reefer. Or Edith's sailor suit emerging as a jumper with a Brigham eyelet guimpe. Or Olive's rose blouse cut into a bolero and ornamented with buttons from Belle (carefully chosen). Whatever it might be, it was, to my eye at least, new, stylish, becoming, offering both the comfort of the familiar and the support of those from whom it had come. One look in the glass and my lassitude left me. I felt equal to anything.

A Time
for Chicken

red to the tradition of thrift, my family set a plain table. Fish was our standby. Cod cost only three cents a pound and haddock four. We could buy clams, already shucked, for fifteen cents a pint. We raised our own vegetables, and at least once a week we served a boiled dinner, a colorful and satisfying concoction of carrots, onions, parsnips, turnips, and potatoes. About as often we had pea soup, cooked thick like porridge, and fried mush, sweetened with syrup made from the sap of our own maples. And, as a matter of course, on Saturday night we had baked beans and brown bread.

We bought little meat. Every family that had a pig slaughtered it as soon as the weather got cold, then smoked the hams, salted the fat, pickled the feet, baked the heart, boiled or fried the liver, and made up all edible scraps into hogshead cheese and sausage. Every family with a hunter in it drew heavily on game: rabbits; partridges — in October and November, you could hardly pass a clump of alders without hearing the brush of their wings; ducks — canvasbacks and mallards had the best flavor because they fed mostly on wild celery; deer.

Only when these supplies were exhausted did we turn to the butcher — we pronounced it "bootyer" — and never then for chicken. According to our tradition, chicken — served so frequently today as to become tedious — was a food for Great Moments. Fourth of July did not warrant it — that was a day for salmon and green peas, anyway — nor Easter, when respectable people ate codfish cakes and hard-boiled eggs served with raw onions soaking in vinegar. Chicken was reserved for Thanksgiving and Christmas. People who had it at any other time without something momentous to celebrate were suspected of High Living.

Thanksgiving and Christmas were both big days. They brought steamed squash, boiled onions, cranberry sauce — we called it cramberry — four kinds of pickles, and three kinds of dessert besides grapes in long, heavy bunches, nuts, and seeded raisins. But all these were as nothing compared to the chicken that graced the head of the table — crisp, brown, savory, redolent of sage and oyster.

We ate all we wanted then, and no one reminded us of the waste there is to a chicken, nor lamented that there should be nothing left over. Ordinarily, leftovers were imperative. (We felt cheated without them. Just as every scrap of cloth went into quilts and holders, so every bit of leftover meat went into hash or pies, every crumb of leftover bread into puddings or dressings.) Moreover,

if it was a hen we were eating, no one sighed over our recklessness in having cut off a source of production. At least twice a year we were openly, blatantly, indulgent.

Yet there were still greater days — oh, perhaps a dozen in a decade — when we had something of import to celebrate. My sister was valedictorian of her class, for instance; my brother was once awarded a medal for bravery. At such a time, we rushed to my father who, being something of a patriarch, made all the decisions for the family. If the news was sufficiently impressive, he would raise his glasses to a convenient crease that held them securely on his forehead, and say in a deep, oratorical voice: "This, I should judge, is a Time for Chicken."

At that we dashed off to place our order with Mrs. Turner, who raised Plymouth Rocks.

Though she appeared to have no special fondness for her chickens, Mrs. Turner did not sell them lightly. First, she had to be acquainted with the occasion. That revealed, she took a large bone hairpin from the enormous pug that topped her head, poked her scalp with it while, frowning, she debated as to whether or not she should spare a young rooster for slaughter. Meanwhile we waited, agonized, sometimes even praying. (Though Mrs. Turner had never refused our family, she had been known to refuse others.)

She always gave in reluctantly, as though she felt duty-bound to discourage such extravagance. But this did not discourage us. Once out of her sight, we spread the news on all sides, making no attempt to conceal our elation. Nor did our listeners attempt to conceal their awe. We were going to have Chicken. It was something to swagger about, and they acknowledged it.

But — let me hasten to say it — whatever the day of the occasion itself, the dinner was always on the following Sunday. To have chicken on a weekday, unless, of course, it was Thanksgiving or Christmas, was unheard of.

Though we were, naturally, impatient, this discrepancy between the event and its consummation made no real difference to us; for, as far as we were concerned, the Great Moment came not on the platform but at the dining-room table when the chicken was brought in.

On such a day, the dinner had none of the holiday fixings. There were no grapes, no nuts, no raisins. But we did not miss them. Just the presence of Chicken itself on our, but no other, table was enough to fill us with wild, weakening excitement.

"Yes," my father would say, picking up the carving-set with visible emotion, while we breathed in the succulent, almost forgotten aroma, "this is, indeed, a Time for Chicken."

I suppose no one ever quite escapes the past. Certainly, I have never been able to do so in the matter of chicken. Once when a neighbor told me, quite unmoved, that she had bought a capon, I startled her by asking what had happened. Since then I have learned to keep silent. On marketing days when my funds are low, I carry home tripe, or liver, or kidneys while my associates, sometimes right in the middle of the week, thank goodness for chicken. But though at such a time my face is composed, my heart is tumultuous, knowing itself in the presence of sacrilege!

The Extraordinary Spring

ocated on an old Indian campsite not far from the center of Blue Hill, it was, indeed, an extraordinary spring. People who had springs of their own — some of more than passing quality — came from miles around in carriages and jiggers bringing buckets to be filled. It was said that no horse in town would willingly have passed the trough supplied by its overflow.

In the lawsuit it was ultimately to provoke, witness after witness gave testimony to its excellence. Mr. Eben Mayo swore it to be "one of the best." Mr. George Morse, who had recently sold his house, asserted that in moving he "didn't calculate to get more than a mile and a half from it." Mrs. Abby Fulton, an early owner of the property, declared that it was the chief inducement for her husband, the village doctor, to choose the place in spite of her objections that it was too far (actually less than a quarter of a mile) from the post office.

It is odd that it should have sustained such appeal, for only a few yards separated it from the old village graveyard. Even in the late 1800s, when this story begins, such a circumstance might have raised questions, especially since in 1865 a cloudburst of historic proportions had hit Blue Hill, washing out bridges and so enlarging the gully between the graveyard and the spring that two coffins had been exposed not far from the spring itself.

Nevertheless its reputation had remained, even increased with time. So great was its popularity that Mr. Thomas Hinckley, who owned or was believed to own the property on which it flowed, began to lose his patience. Wanting to wash his carriages at the trough at his own convenience, he often found himself frustrated by long lines of thirsty horses and bucket-laden men. Finally, exasperated, he covered and padlocked the spring. The lock was promptly broken. The lines resumed. Essentially a philosophical man, he gave up completely.

His heirs were equally philosophical. They must have been generous, too, for they allowed my father who, after tasting the water from the spring, had become disenchanted with that from our own quite adequate well, to dig another spring beside it. Fed from the same source, it was easily piped into our house, which was separated from the Hinckleys' only by the house of Captain Spencer Treworgy. All was tranquil until the arrival of Reverend C. M. G. Harwood.

Just when he came or where he came from is not clear. We knew only that, as a retired minister of great dignity and presence, he had preached mostly in the West (which to us meant anywhere beyond Massachusetts). Where he and Miss Treworgy met remains a complete mystery. It is possible he had first come to Blue Hill as one of the long line of substitute preachers who had occupied the pulpit for a Sunday or two, as indistinguishable one

from another as a single crow in a flock. Or it is possible that she met him in either Skowhegan or Eastport where he held brief pastorates, though the county paper makes no mention of her having visited either town. The place of the marriage is also unknown, but the time must have been around 1880, for she was not listed as a resident of Blue Hill in the census of that year. Her age was then forty-one.

Miss Treworgy had long been known to the genteel of the village as a "maiden lady." To the unmannered young, she was simply an "old maid." The idea that she had a husband, any husband at all, seemed preposterous, even indecent. Indeed, many did not believe it until she returned with him in or about 1895.

To the astonishment of the village, the Reverend Harwood was a fine figure of a man. Clearly younger than his wife, he was tall with broad shoulders, heavy white hair, and a neat mustache. His clothes were always pressed, his collar spotless, his shoes well-shined. No matter what he was doing, feeding the pig or substituting in the pulpit, where his deep, bass voice was equally melodious in hymn or prayer, his appearance was impeccable.

The few who scoffed (mostly the barbershop loafers) focused on his name, insisting that the initials C. M. G. stood for Clement Marmeduke Gabriel. Clement was undoubtedly correct, for it appears on his burial certificate. There are some who still believe in the authenticity of Marmeduke and Gabriel. The Reverend Harwood himself gave no clue. Nor does his tombstone.

He must soon have found time hanging heavy on his hands, for he was often seen wandering out-of-doors, especially in the Treworgy pasture which lay across the street from their house and adjacent to the spring. On these occasions he always carried a yardstick. Obviously he was investigating their boundaries. He soon announced that the spring was not on the Hinckley property at all, but on land belonging to the town. That being true, he was as free as my father, he claimed, to profit from it. The Treworgys already had a spring in their own pasture, a spring as good as most, but he presumably had tasted the magic water and coveted more.

When his argument fell on deaf ears, trouble began between our two families. Up to this time the Harwoods had spoken to us, albeit coolly, in passing. They now passed in silence. The shades in the windows facing our house were drawn. But it was early in the 1900s, when our family put in a bathroom, that the real trouble began. Our water supply diminished, presumably by nightly bailings; a cover which my father placed on the spring was broken and the water routinely riled. The Reverend Harwood and my father, both speakers of local renown, refused to appear on the same platform together.

This turn of events was a source of great concern to my mother. She tried to keep the particulars from the older children — this was before my birth — but, very conscious of the breach, they welcomed the excitement it brought. A neighbor tells how, on one of the guided tours to our bathroom — so frequent as to preclude its usefulness to the family — one of my sisters, eight years old at the time, pointed to the hot-water faucet closest to the Harwoods and whispered solemnly, "*H* is for Harwood." Then indicating the other on the opposite side of the bowl, she added, "And *C* is for Chase."

But as the older children's understanding increased, so did their fervor. Familiar with Mary Lamb's tales from Shakespeare, they saw themselves in the tradition of the Montagues and the Capulets; and, while careful to keep out of our mother's hearing, they stood just inside the kitchen windows, shouting, with appropriate gesture, the words of the feuding servants in the story: "I bite my thumb at you!"

In 1904 my father, taking an early morning stroll, apprehended Brooks Gray, a laborer hired by the Harwoods, in the act of digging a trench to deflect our water's flow. Indignant, he argued the Hinckley heirs, themselves indifferent to the situation and by this time widely scattered, into taking the case to court, with him as their attorney, in an attempt to establish forever the family claim, but principally, of course, his own.

The case was heard in 1905. During its procedure my father, agitated, inadvertently revealed what he was up to, and the judge, annoyed with both parties, dismissed the case. "Settle it between yourselves," he said.

After the trial things quieted down considerably. It was a time of watchful waiting. The Reverend Harwood placed an enormous "No Trespassing" sign in his pasture, set directly to face our house. (This seemed unnecessary since we had never felt inclined to go there.) My father put a heavy metal cover with padlock on our spring. My mother, fearful of some new provocation, began secretly to draw, except for drinking, our water from the well again. Things seemed almost normal.

Then one Sunday in the early fall of 1909 while we were eating dinner we heard a loud knock on the window facing the Treworgy house. Looking up, we saw the Reverend Harwood's white face peering in and heard his deep voice intone one word: "Fire!"

Now, in our village we dreaded no disaster so much as fire. Storms, even hurricanes, we could handily weather. Blizzards did not faze us, nor did drought, though it took patience sometimes to wait one out. Sickness we took for granted. But fire was another matter. Our only method of fighting it was a village bucket brigade, summoned by the ringing of the church bell. This had limited success, especially during the hunting season or when fish were running in the bay.

My father, who believed in being prepared for anything, had organized the entire family into our own fire brigade and given each of us specific instructions for procedure. He and my brother would rush for the ladder kept against the wall just inside the barn door; my mother would seize the big bag of salt, used to douse chimney fires, that hung by the grain bin; each sister would steadily grasp one of the buckets of well water, always filled and set handily in an empty stall; I, the youngest, and in all practical matters retarded, would be best kept out of the way by bringing two heavy bath towels soaked at the kitchen sink, in case someone should require resuscitation. Thus equipped, we would fall into a procession led by my father and immediately begin action. So when we heard the dreaded word we responded instantly.

But things did not go quite the way my father had planned. A carriage left too close to the door impeded agility with the ladder. The twine suspending the bag of salt had rotted, breaking under the force of my mother's hand; fortunately the bag itself remained intact. One bucket, almost empty, suggested that a thirsty cow had paused to refresh herself as she passed. Only I, perhaps seven at the time, had met no obstacle and stood smugly, shamelessly enjoying it all. What would be the appropriate words to speak as I revived a half-conscious victim, especially a mortal enemy? Would it be "Fear not! I shall save you"? Or perhaps "Behold, we have come in your hour of need"? It was hard to decide.

By the time we were finally off, the smell of smoke

was already in the air. Our progress was slow, hampered by the shrubbery and the necessity to skirt my mother's jealously guarded petunias. The smoke grew heavy.

The Treworgy house was a hundred feet above our own on the crest of a steep banking. Still in formation, we slipped and stumbled to the top. The Reverend Harwood had disappeared. Though the smoke was darkening steadily, we could not see its source. My mother set down the bag of salt and rang the bell. There was no answer. She rang again. No sound anywhere.

They were all overcome, I told myself, delighted. All, all lying unconscious. The Reverend Harwood had gone back in to rescue the others and had himself fallen. There would be a medal in it for me. Gold, of course, and since three would have been rescued, no doubt a diamond.

Getting no response to the bell, my mother had begun desperately to pound on the door. "Come out, come out," she called. Still no response. She turned the knob, or tried to, but the door was locked from the inside. She pounded harder. "Come out. Come out," she kept repeating.

"Come out, come out," I echoed, extending the dripping towels. "Come out before it is too late!" Hearing the commotion, my father descended the ladder from which he had been inspecting the roof. It was then that he saw, through the steadily thickening smoke, flames spurting high from our *own* chimney.

For the first time in my life I heard him swear. Then, recovering, he picked up one end of the ladder. My brother seized the other and we dashed, formation forgotten, down the banking and through the shrubbery, trampling heedlessly on the cherished garden. My father and brother set up the ladder. My mother readied the salt. My sisters rushed to the well to refill the almost empty buckets.

Drenched and disconsolate, a heroine no longer, I soberly laid the soggy, grimy towels over the mangled petunias.

The damage to the house was inconsequential, and for a time things went on as before, the same drawn shades, the same public snubbings from the Harwoods. There was, however, a change in Blue Hill itself. Grown soft or more fastidious, more people began to demand bathrooms. This meant artesian wells, abundance of water seeming more desirable than quality. As a result, there was a gradual drop in the water level of the village. Springs lowered precariously, sometimes dried up. Daily we could watch the Reverend Harwood cross his pasture, presumably to inspect theirs. Our own remained remarkably stable.

It may have been for this reason alone that around 1912 tension again mounted. Though there was nothing you could put your finger on, you could feel it in the air. "Look out and see what's going on," my father would say to one of us, meaning, of course, look in the direction of the Treworgys. Sometimes in looking we could detect a movement of a shade, indicating that one of them was spying, too. This generated considerable excitement. When a day was particularly dull, we would take a drink of water from the faucet, loudly pronounce ourselves poisoned and writhe, groaning, upon the kitchen floor until my mother came to put a stop to it.

But it was not until 1914, six weeks before my father's death, that a crisis — the real crisis — came. The Hinckley heirs finally got together and decided to sell their property, quietly offering it to my mother. Distraught as she was by my father's illness, she decided to buy, knowing it was something he himself would have done to better establish his claim to the spring.

The results were almost immediate. My brother, by

this time a sturdy young man in his early twenties, looked out very early one morning to see a large pile of gravel beside the spring, with Mrs. Harwood, then seventy-five and very frail, busily shoveling from it into what appeared to be a large hole in the well's metal cover. He hurried to the scene. Arrived, he bent to examine the hole, allowing Mrs. Harwood a fine opportunity to hit him on his head with her shovel. He turned, seized her lightly around the waist (she was so small his fingers met) and set her neatly on the edge of the watering trough. Then as he bent to pick up the crowbar with which she had made the hole, a gesture which she interpreted as threatening, she broke the long silence with a shrill, continous scream. He headed for home. Before night he was served a subpoena, charged with assault and battery.

The hearing, for such it turned out to be, was public, with most of the town present, while our family, except for the accused, remained at home, sitting discreetly in the parlor. The Harwoods were represented by a lawyer "from away." My brother handled his own case, his plea being self-defense. He was a young man of keen wit who had long since seen the absurdity of the entire situation. No records exist, but those who were present tell me there was never a funnier show in town. Once again there was no verdict, and it broke up in general laughter.

According to the undertaker's records, the Reverend Harwood died on Christmas Day, 1916, though the inscription on his stone reads a year later. He and my father lie in the graveyard by the shore, the same distance apart as in life, while the extraordinary spring, supplanted, diminished, half-hidden by weeds and bushes, flows on.

Once,
at Christmas

This is the story about a Christmas long ago. It was not such a Christmas as children dream about. To be sure, there was a tree, but it was a scrawny, shapeless one, clearly chosen by indifferent eyes, and set up, not in the warm comfort of a parlor, but in the dim, drafty cellar of a village hotel.

There were no candles. The only light came from smoky lanterns brought in from the shed, the only music from a string of rusty sleigh bells. There were no candy bags, no festoons of popcorn and cranberries. The presents didn't amount to much. Most of them were practical things we would have had anyway sooner or later — sweaters, mittens, stocking caps. The others, homemade, were for the most part unrecognizable. Conspicuously missing was a hearth to gather around, where we could feel relaxed and secure and united. In its place was a great, threatening steam furnace whose workings no one on the premises understood.

Yet that Christmas was the happiest of my childhood. But to tell about it, I must first tell other things.

My father was a country lawyer and proud of his calling, but he liked to fancy himself a businessman as well. So, as he drove almost daily between the courthouse in Ellsworth and our home in Blue Hill, he was constantly spotting property which he believed had investment possibilities and too often buying it. Most of these investments proved worthless. One was disastrous.

This was our village hotel. An enormous four-story building backed by a livery stable, it stood directly at the head of the town landing. Two piazzas, one above the other, ran on three sides, to some extent mitigating its ugliness. Built in 1825 for a village store, it was remodeled into a hotel in the late eighties when a brief mining boom hit the coast. In 1905, when my father took it over, it had already defeated a series of owners.

It should be said at once in his defense that he had never expected his family to live there, for he was as aware as was my mother, who had vigorously opposed its purchase, of the shadowy reputation of the place, a reputation begun when the town had been cluttered with strangers and money flowed fast. Indeed, he had assured her over and over that there would be no occasion for any of us ever to go inside. He intended, he explained, to hire a manager from away who would bring his own staff.

He did, and once again history began to repeat itself.

As one manager followed another, the debt at the bank grew. When, in 1907, the entire staff left without warning, taking much that was portable with them, my mother, for the first time since her marriage, gave an ultimatum. We would close our house and move to the hotel. She herself would get the place on its feet.

My father protested, argued, stormed, but eventually gave in. "Well, I suppose," he granted, "since it will be only a matter of weeks. A couple of months, at most."

We stayed five years.

On a visit of inspection, my mother was relieved by what she saw. The kitchen was passable, largely because of a dumbwaiter that connected it with the dining area. The halls were decently carpeted. The bedrooms had neat straw matting upon their floors. Except in the office where the heavy, pretentious mahogany of mining days remained, the furniture was of golden oak. There were two bathrooms, each equipped with a tin-lined tub and a flush pulled by a chain. She must have been especially relieved to find the parlor, reputedly the center of high living, equipped with stiff, high-backed chairs, and a prim, narrow settee which would have discouraged sin.

We moved in late summer — my parents, my sister, ten, my brother, seven, and I, just past five. Our luggage was scanty. "We'll be home in no time," my mother said brightly. "Anyway, by Christmas."

Poor Mama. She really believed it.

My mother's first move had been to hire native help. Arriving early was Mrs. Guptill, the cook, neat as a pin and, incidentally, built almost like one. She was sharp as a pin, too. No one ever put anything over on Mrs. Guptill. Her thrift was a thing to marvel at. If my mother said, "I think we will need a gallon of vinegar," Mrs. Guptill was sure, quick as a flash, to correct her. "Not a whole gallon," she would say, protesting. "Half will do." It was the same with everything: half a barrel, half a bushel, half a pint. Once when my father sent down word that a pig should be killed for Thanksgiving, she was almost frantic. "Not a

whole pig," she cried. She never wasted anything. Once she put five cough drops into a fruitcake she was making just because "they were lying around useless."

Ada, her assistant, had a broad, shining face, brown eyes, and light brown hair which she wore in a pompadour with the aid of a wire frame. Nothing bothered Ada: not a spilled cup of coffee, not a transient coming in at seven o'clock, not twenty-eight lamps to clean daily. All she asked was an hour off in the afternoon so that she could study up on the *Lovers' Guide and Manual* which she kept hidden behind the dinner plates. For Ada had her dreams. Her ideal was an older man — a gentleman, she emphasized, with a white mustache. Preferably an Englishman who dropped his *h*'s. Since there was no one in town who approximated this, she tolerated the attention of Benjamin, the stableman.

Benjamin was big, blond, and slow-speaking. He knew all there was to know about horses. No horse he trained ever shied twice at an automobile. Though he used the whip at times, he had a way horses responded to. No one ever got the better of him on a trade. Knowing his worth, he took orders from no one. "Do this," my father would say, or "Do that." Benjamin would listen with an air of respect, but he would do exactly as he pleased, and both of them knew it. On the other hand, he was quick to act on any suggestion of my mother and would have done so even had it been against his better judgment.

His helper was Basil Googins, generally referred to as Boshy. Boshy was a little man with no chin, and shoulders so shapeless that the straps of his overalls were forever slipping off them. His face had nothing whatever in it but two eyes, a nose, and a mouth; even the flesh and bone were meager. The most conspicuous thing about him was a sniff that came regularly. *One, two, three, sniff. One, two, three, sniff.* You could detect any slackening in its tempo

45

as you can a clock running down. Mrs. Guptill bullied him disgracefully.

We got off to a good start. As word of the hotel spread, drummers who normally made their headquarters in Ellsworth changed them to Blue Hill. Other transients came — visiting ministers, door-to-door salesmen, itinerant photographers. (Ping-pong pictures were just coming in.) A dentist serving in the area took over the parlor every Friday, using the organ stool borrowed from the church vestry for his chair. Praise of Mrs. Guptill's cooking, with its unique and mysterious flavors, quickened the dining-room trade.

Until early October we managed to keep warm with the heat from the kitchen, which drifted up the dumb-waiter, and from stoves in the office and parlor. But by the middle of the month, drafts edged in, sneaking around corners. Clearly some action had to be taken.

Half of the ground floor was taken up by the kitchen; the other half held a monstrous furnace, bordered by rows of cordwood which nearly reached the ceiling. Though there were other furnaces in town, probably half a dozen of them, they were all of the hot-air variety. This one heated by steam. No one on the place knew how to work its multiplicity of drafts, dampers, and gauges. The town plumber was on his prolonged annual vacation. My father, completely helpless when faced with demands for manual skill, suddenly remembered urgent business in Augusta and turned the entire matter over to Benjamin.

Not over-pleased, Benjamin began to push and pull and pound with such vehemence that my mother, terrified, begged him to stop. If there was to be an explosion, she declared, she preferred to be the one responsible.

First she had Boshy fill all the buckets on the premises

from the watering trough in the stable and set them around the furnace. Then she sent out warning of the impending disaster. Mrs. Guptill, unperturbed, continued to roll out pastry for her six daily pies. Ada, her eyes covered by her apron, fled to the stable. We children were sternly banished to the end of the landing, where, presumably, should the building blow up, we could save ourselves by jumping into the bay. Then, with Benjamin loyally beside her, my mother struck the first match.

The fire sputtered, burned grudgingly, and eventually, following a great clatter in the pipes, sent out a little heat. Benjamin discreetly added one stick after another while my mother, beside him, urged restraint. Soon the arrow on the central gauge began moving upward. Then and there my mother decided arbitrarily upon a point it must not pass. She decided, too, that when the fire was really going it must constantly be watched. So each of us, family and help alike, was assigned a time for watching. My time was from three to four in the afternoon.

I was not afraid, for someone was always within call. But it was dull and dark in the cellar. The earthen floor chilled my feet. There was only one window and it was low and dusty. Through it I could see only feet: Benjamin's lumberman's rubbers, trailing a little straw; Boshy's moccasins, broken down at the heel; Ada's high-button boots, picking their way. Sitting there on the ragged chopping block, I sometimes tried to scare myself just to make things livelier. The place was sure to blow up. Didn't my mother expect it? I remembered a book in our library at home that told about Vesuvius and Pompeii, especially about the bodies that had been found there. Some had been curled in sleep; some had covered their faces in fear. I would not be caught napping, I determined. My face would show no fright. They would find me folding my hands in prayer,

47

or perhaps shielding my eyes with my hand to show that I had died still watching. I practiced both gestures over and over, trying to decide between them.

But most of the time I just thought about home where there was a furnace that behaved itself and where your feet were never cold. Where you could stand right on a register and let your skirts balloon around you. Where there were no pipes to pound and clatter. No arrows that had to be watched . . . .

Then I would begin to count off the days until Christmas. Thirty-four, thirty-three, thirty . . . . And all the time the arrow would be mounting. "Come, Mama. Come *quick*!" She would rush in, cheeks flushing, open doors, and shut off dampers. "Thank goodness we caught it in time," she would always exclaim when the crisis had passed.

Only one part of the hotel was tolerable to us children. That was the kitchen. It had a landing on its stairs where we could crouch, safely out of the way yet able to see and hear all that went on below: Mrs. Guptill kneading the twelve loaves of bread she baked daily, or rolling out yard after yard of pastry, hoarding all scraps; Ada skimming off thick blankets of cream or setting and resetting the long table where people ate at all hours — transients too late for the dining room; itinerants who couldn't pay the thirty-five cents required for a meal there; stage drivers who kept their horses in the stable. Better still, we could listen to the talk that went on, the nature of which my mother never knew. Talk about drownings, murders, apparitions. We found it very satisfying.

In one corner of the room was a pump with a rusty base and a long wooden handle. It was the heart of the hotel, for only by its manipulation — forward, backward, forward, backward — hour in and hour out, could we exist

48

at all. It took a strong man to work it, for the water had to go from the well by the furnace to a huge zinc-lined tank on the fourth floor. Often men from the village would drop in after supper and give Benjamin a hand.

This was especially true on Saturday nights when one of Ada's five indistinguishable brothers brought in the family phonograph. As word of this spread, pumping no longer became a problem. A long line formed at the foot of the stairs, ready to seize the handle and move it in rhythm to the music. "Arra Wanna, on my honor . . ." Except for Mrs. Guptill, the entire audience joined in on the chorus.

Among the songs there was one outstanding favorite:

> My wife's gone to the country
> Hoo-ray! Hoo-ray!
> She thought it best to take a rest
> Hoo-ray! Hoo-ray!
> She took the children with her
> Hoo-ray! Hoo-ray! . . .

Eventually there was a gurgle in the sink, meaning that the tank was full. Then came the noisiest, rowdiest chorus of all:

> I love my wife but oh, you kid,
> My wife's gone away . . . .

At this point my mother left her accounts to appear suddenly and discover us, clapping and stamping with the others. "Bedtime," she said emphatically, and rushed us off to say our prayers.

Thanksgiving passed, December came, and still there was no snow. The air grew cold, colder. My mother and Ada put hot soapstones in all the beds at night. When we dragged ourselves from the covers in the morning, the outdoor thermometer often shivered between ten and twenty below. The ruts in the roads were frozen so solid that we wrenched our ankles and bit our tongues as we stumbled our way to school.

It was rough going even for the horses. Passengers on the stage were expected to get off and walk up hills since, with Christmas not far ahead, the loads were getting heavy. It was slow going, too. Sometimes packages jounced off and had to be retrieved. Everyone was jittery. Everyone but us children, for we would be home soon, wouldn't we? Hadn't we been promised?

Our wagons, which should long ago have been replaced by pungs, began to show the strain. On the tenth of the month the tongue of the biggest revealed a crack which the blacksmith repaired with an iron band; on the fifteenth a spring broke. With the biggest loads still ahead, this meant only one thing — a new wagon.

Our financial situation had continued to improve. With traveling bad, transients stayed longer. Two Saturdays a month the local representative of a corset company rented No. 10 (the only bedroom with a lock) and, as double protection, set up a screen, behind which she made her measurements. Two of the teachers would come as regular boarders when the winter term began. According to my father, the new manager would be well broken in by then. Now this.

Its full impact did not strike my sister and me until the morning of the twenty-first when my mother came into our room and found us packing. "We won't be going home just yet," she began lamely.

We listened, first stunned, then angry. "But you promised," we chorused accusingly. "You *promised.*"

The new wagon must be bought at once, she explained. There wouldn't be money enough for that and to hire a manager as well. We would have to stay a little longer. It would be a different kind of Christmas. That was all. It would be a nice change to see the tree set up in a hotel parlor.

We didn't think it would be nice at all and said so vehemently. Then we began sulking, refusing to eat dinner, refusing even to leave our room. That night my father brought our supper on a tray. This was such a reversal of the way things were done in our family that, taken aback, we did not even thank him.

But the next morning, remembering the guilt and misery we had seen in his face, we softened enough to go out and cut a tree. We did not search the pastures, comparing this one and that. We took the first one we came across. It didn't amount to much, but it seemed good enough for a hotel parlor.

Before we were up on the twenty-second, my father had started off. Normally he drove Alice, a mare he himself had bred, but the rough roads had lamed her. Instead, he took Frisky, hardly more than a filly and still in the process of training. He would stable her in Ellsworth and catch the morning train to Thomaston. As a trustee of the State Prison there, he was determined to buy the wagon in its workshop. He would return on the morning of the twenty-fourth, pick up Frisky at the stable, and be home in time for a late dinner.

Late in the morning of the twenty-fourth snow began falling. At first it came slowly, feeling its way. Then, suddenly as the wind rose, it came faster, until, watching from the office window, my sister and I saw it reach the ankles of the passers-by. My mother left the desk, where she had been working on the accounts, to watch the arrow on the furnace. Every few minutes she came back upstairs to look at the clock. Urged on by her, my sister and I went halfheartedly to hang the decorations on the tree, which Boshy had set up in the parlor. By the time we had finished and looked out again, we could see nothing but snow. It was as though, hoarded for weeks, it had been suddenly spilled and dispersed by a whirlwind.

At first she did not speak. Then my sister said soberly, "I wonder where Papa is."

I had been wondering that, too.

My father had just passed the East Surry post office when the first flakes fell. He had returned by train to Ellsworth, taken the hack to the American House where he had breakfast. Then he had gone up to the courthouse on an errand, which took longer than expected, so that it was almost eleven when he hitched Frisky to the buggy and started for home.

The snow surprised him, for an early look at the sky had shown nothing unusual. He now knew that he must either go back and wait until the ground was well-covered and then change to a sleigh, or give Frisky her head. He chose the latter. If the snow didn't let up, he would stop at the store in Surry and call Benjamin, he decided. But when he got there, he found the store had already closed for the holiday. There was only one other telephone between Surry and Blue Hill. That was at Lote Cushman's, three miles ahead. He could make it easily in half an hour.

The traveling proved harder than he had thought. Being loose and moist, the snow clung to the rims of the wheels, adding its weight. It clung to Frisky's hooves, too, slowing progress. She grew fretful, veering sharply at each gust of wind. When the muscles in her back began to show signs of strain, my father pulled up every now and then to give her a rest. A quarter of a mile from Cushman's, he got out and walked to lighten her load. Once there, he tied her to the gatepost and waded up the long drive.

Dinner over, the Cushmans — a dozen or so of them — had begun decorating their tree. Of course he could use the telephone, Lote told him, if it was working. It wasn't. The line was down already. He was careful not to tell his predicament lest Lote offer to hitch up and take him home. (My father was not one to disrupt a family celebration.) Urged to eat something, he took only a cup of coffee, and started down the drive. When, breathless and chilled, he got to the gate, he found that Frisky and the buggy had disappeared.

As the office clock struck three, my mother went into the kitchen and found Ada and Mrs. Guptill sitting silently together at the table. "Benjamin will take you home now," she told them. "I'll send word to the stable." She had already given them their presents, wishing they might have been more. But they refused. "We're waiting here until Mr. Chase gets back," Mrs. Guptill said with finality. And Ada nodded her head so violently in agreement that her wire framework slipped a little.

At four, Boshy and my brother came into the parlor, saying that my mother had sent them to bring down the tree. It was to be set up in the cellar so that we could keep an eye on the arrow and still be together on Christmas Eve.

We stood silent and unbelieving, staring scornfully at the tree as they struggled to get it upright through the door. When they were gone, we burst into tears of rage. It had been bad enough to think of Christmas in a hotel parlor, but in a cellar! The disgrace of it! Everyone in town would know. No one would ever speak to us again.

"I hate Papa," my sister shouted.

"So do I," I echoed. And, not to be outdone, I added, "I hate Mama, too."

Together we raced down to proclaim it, but before we could speak Benjamin appeared in the doorway.

53

"Frisky's back," he said, "and there's nobody with her."
We watched my mother's face whiten. Then Benjamin
spoke again. "We'll be startin' right off, ma'am. Boshy's
hitchin' one of the workhorses to the pung."

My father had set off walking, confident that someone would come along and give him a lift, for the snow
had eased a bit, though the wind seemed stronger. Having
been sheltered by the buggy and warmed momentarily by
the coffee, he had not until then realized the full force of
the cold. It scorched his throat and lungs; it burned his
ears and numbed his fingers. The weight of his boots grew
heavier. Still he plodded on, alert for the sound of bells.
He could, at most, see only two or three feet ahead.

By the time he had gone half a mile, his fingers began
to stiffen. He flexed them, then took off his gloves and
blew on his knuckles, breathing heavily. Still wading, for
the snow was above his boot tops, he tried to put his gloves
back on again. In doing it, he dropped one and, bending
in a vain effort to retrieve it, he stumbled against a rock,
almost a boulder. He knew then that he was no longer on
the road but in a pasture.

He wiped the snow from his eyes and peered for
landmarks. None. He looked for his tracks, but they had
already filled. For the first time he felt real apprehension.
Which way should he head? He could tell nothing from
the wind, for it was coming in every direction.

While he stood there, tense and undecided, a great
gust ripped off his cap and almost knocked him over.
Bracing against it, he could not feel his feet any longer.
His arms began to shake. His legs. His whole body.

He knew that he must keep moving. Bending painfully, with bare hands he pushed the snow from his legs
where it had almost reached his knees, and struggled to

54

take a step forward. Instead, he felt himself sinking. The brook? A gully?

He felt panic. He opened his mouth and with stiffened jaws began shouting. It was then, right then, that, far off, distorted by the wind, he heard Benjamin's strong voice: "Hallooo. Hallooo."

Much later in the evening when the stars were out and the wind had stopped blowing, Mrs. Guptill and Ada, who had again refused to leave, prepared a lavish supper on the big kitchen table. "Plenty and to spare," Mrs. Guptill announced when we, having been told to wait until we were called, at last filed down the stairs. And plenty there was! Ham, cold tongue, hogshead cheese, mashed potatoes, hot biscuits, cabbage salad, pickled beets, jellies, preserves, three kinds of pie. "Don't scrimp now," Mrs. Guptill admonished as, astonished, we pulled out our chairs.

My father, both hands frostbitten and bandaged, his legs wrapped in a blanket, sat at the head of the table and told for the first time, but in a voice not yet quite his own, the complete story. Nobody said much. Emotions were well covered up in our family. Instead, with one of us carrying my father's chair, we all trooped into the cellar, Benjamin leading the way.

All was warmth and fragrance there. Lanterns hung from the rafters cast a soft light on the tree, looking no longer scrawny but in its shadowy surroundings shining like a tree from fairyland. It stood on the well-curb, and we sat in a circle around it — all nine of us, not now family and help, but friends, as we were always to be.

Led by Ada and Benjamin, we sang all the carols we knew, Mrs. Guptill surprising us with a fine soprano. Sitting beside her, Boshy played an accompaniment on a string of rusty sleigh bells, his sniff following the rhythm. Then my mother handed my father an open Bible and, still wrapped in his blanket, he read aloud to us the familiar story of another Christmas, in a stable.

Cousin My

ousin My lived on a farm five miles north of the village. She did not live there by choice, for it was isolated, and more than anyone I have ever known she hated solitude. For years she had tried to get her husband to move to the village, but he was considerably older than she and not given to change. After his death she had not been able to sell the farm, and because of her limited income was obliged to stay there. She was a shrewd woman, and in addition to raising her vegetables she had planted a large patch of fine raspberries, rare and highly valued in our parts. After selling a few crates of them to a merchant from Bangor, she distributed the remainder gratuitously to favored people in the village, using our house as her center for distribution.

Though related — indeed, if related at all — on my father's side of the family, it was my mother who had to put up with her. For as soon as she arrived, my father invariably remembered some mysterious business which would take him out of town.

Cousin My was a great talker, and most of her talk concerned funerals. Since she had a horse and buggy to transport her, she took in every one within the radius of fifteen miles and never missed a detail. Not only did she report the attire of the deceased and the color of the casket and its lining (plain or pleated) but the exact number of floral tributes, since she managed by frequent changing of seat to work her way to a position of advantage.

If now and then she failed on the exact message on a card or the count of a spray of carnations, she never failed in any detail of the procession. She knew the exact number of surreys, buggies, and carriages, or, as the case might be, cutters and pungs. She knew who rode in each, who did or did not wear veils, even the number of hand-kerchiefs exposed on the way. For Cousin My, the proces-sion was the highest point in any funeral, indeed, of any life. Her esteem for the deceased depended not on his obituary nor the size of his monument, but upon the number of vehicles that followed him to the grave.

Much of her time was spent in reviewing her own "arrangements." She sat in a rocker on our back piazza, pale, stocky, her fading hair darkened at the part and temples with tea, edging her chair ever closer to my mother's. Her voice, disciplined to funerals, had become habitually lowered. But though banished to the barn or kitchen, we children managed to hear a good deal.

Her funeral was to be held in her parlor. Folding chairs were to be borrowed from the Grange. Her under-things (wrapped in blue tissue paper) were in her second bureau drawer. Her black dress with its lavender fichu hung, unworn, in the spare closet and might need to be taken in should she suffer long. Her black shoes, kept well-shined, were beneath it. My mother, resigned, would listen, nodding and giving reassuring pats on Cousin My's

thighs, so plump it did not seem to us, eavesdropping, that even prolonged suffering could diminish them much.

"I do wish My would have her funeral in the church," my mother once complained to my father upon his cautious return. "She's been a member for years. Besides, it's the natural place with the graveyard so close by. It's a lot to expect of people, taking that long trek to the farm."

My father's eyes twinkled as he refilled his dish with raspberries. "If you haven't figured that out, you're not as smart as I thought you were," he said. "People will go, and they will have to come back, won't they?"

She granted it.

"And how else but in the procession?" he demanded. "It'll be the longest procession this town has ever known. And mark my word, My's been planning on that for twenty years. Did you ever know her to give raspberries to anyone without a horse?"

We were all familiar with the procession and its protocol. Our carriage (we being, she asserted, next of kin) would lead it, directly following the hearse. Behind us would come the minister and the deacons; then the members of the Missionary Society; then the Relief Corps; then the Rebekahs; then the mourners, church members having priority. It would proceed to the village, avoiding the short cut — she was most particular about this — and follow the main street to the graveyard, where her stone, except for the fateful date, had long been standing

Cousin My died suddenly in 1910 on the day after Thanksgiving. My sisters were home from college, and my parents, taking advantage of this, had just left town for a few days in Boston. When the news came, my sisters, bossy by nature, declared that under no circumstances were they to be recalled. They themselves would manage everything. One would oversee the arrangements so often outlined, the other would lead the procession, following the hearse.

Now my father had, as was his custom, driven to Ellsworth and left his horse in the stable before taking the train. That meant that a horse must be rented from the local livery stable.

The only available one was a nag called Nellie, a spiritless mare with sagging back, drooping head, and clouded eyes. My sister accepted her reluctantly, but there was, she granted, one advantage. Since she was an inexperienced driver, a horse like Nellie would at least be easily managed.

The funeral went exactly as it had been planned. Had she been there in spirit as well as in flesh, Cousin My herself could have found no flaw. But by the time the texts had been read, the prayers spoken, and her virtues extolled, with emphasis upon her generosity, the sky had darkened visibly.

The procession lined up hurriedly, but with careful attention to protocol. For perhaps half a mile all was as it should be. Nellie was the model of equine decorum. The minister and deacons, their heads respectfully bowed, contemplated their mittens, the mourners following suit. Then a few early snowflakes began to fall.

The hearse quickened its speed. My sister slapped the reins on Nellie's sagging back. There was no response. She gave a subdued cluck or two, then another futile slap. Nervously she turned and looked behind. The minister and deacons were as tranquil as ever, seemingly oblivious to the quickening flakes.

She applied the whip gently. Still no action. She tried again, this time with force. Nellie shook, staggered, and started suddenly forward with a speed quite unsuitable for the occasion. Dismayed, my sister pulled the reins. Nellie slowed, then reared abruptly. Then her head jerked downward snapping the checkrein.

My sister looked behind again through the thickening snow but saw no sign of perturbation. She was tempted to call for help, but decorum restrained her. She peered ahead. The hearse was steadily gaining.

Without the checkrein Nellie's behavior grew more erratic. She shook. She staggered. She stopped still, then started up again, weaving a little. Clutching the reins, my sister grew desperate. Suppose Nellie started to run away . . . Suppose, with flying hooves, she passed the hearse, crowding if off the road . . . Suppose, shaken by the rutted roads a wheel flew off . . .

Then she had an inspiration. Just ahead was a cross road that led away from the village. She would maneuver Nellie on that road and thus drop out of the procession, leaving the others to catch up with the hearse.

Somehow, with Nellie stumbling, weaving, she did it. Then she herself began to shake and sweat and shiver. Would Nellie start up again? If she did, and bolted, where would they end? It was a lonely road. Where it went she did not know. If she was thrown out, mutilated, would someone ever find her?

They had gone almost a mile with Nellie subdued but still weaving a little, before it occurred to her to look behind. When she did, she saw to her horror that the entire procession, having lost sight of the hearse in the snow squall, had trustingly followed her, leaving Cousin My to make her last, momentous journey alone.

Black Sunday

 ur village was, by and large, a tolerant one. Politics offered no grounds for dissension, Republicans outnumbering Democrats fifty to one. Pornography was never an issue with us, and the obscenities that appeared in public places were generally ignored. A certain amount of vandalism, we told ourselves, had to be expected, especially on the night before the Fourth, and when swing-chairs and settees disappeared from lawns and piazzas to reappear atop some outhouse or on an island in the bay, we blamed their owners for carelessness in leaving them outside.

When feuds sprang up, as they did now and then over boundaries or lobster pots or trespassing cows, only the parties involved got much upset. For the rest of us they offered real diversion. Yet we were careful not to provoke confrontation and cheerfully acted as inter-mediaries when communication was necessary. All in all, we took things pretty much as they came. When a newly married couple surprised us with a baby, we were bound to do a little quick mental arithmetic, but only the gossips counted out loud. And as for the gossips themselves, we regarded them lightly.

Rowdiness, too, we accepted as a matter of course, especially at Fair time when liquor invariably leaked in (Maine was, of course, a Prohibition state), or on those nights when the steamer lay over and the boat fellows lined the drugstore steps making inflammatory remarks at those who passed. Then if things got really bad, somebody might go far enough to call the constable, who took his time coming, confident that order would be self-imposed before his arrival.

Granted there were times when our patience was strained. A thief who was caught and proved without contrition might be sent away for a few weeks to the State Reform School where it was assumed he would learn a lesson. If he didn't and was caught again, he might end up for a month or so in the County Jail where discipline was known to be casual.

Behavior which today would be termed psychotic we called "just odd." If the man who brought us our clams wanted to board up his windows and live in darkness, that was his business. If two sisters who could never agree painted half the outside of their house yellow and half green, well, that was up to them. Of course if a man chased his neighbor with a hatchet and persisted in it, he might as a last resort be sent for a spell to the asylum in Bangor while, more likely than not, his intended victim kept watch over his place and his family until the time of his release. Generally we lived and let live, even in the matter of religion.

We had two churches, the Congregationalist and the Baptist. There was inevitably some competition between them, and since my father (or more aptly his family) belonged to the former and my mother to the latter, she was careful to allot each of her children to one or the other in turn. Though the Baptists, with whom my lot fell, were the more orthodox, I met only one bigot among them. I was eight years old at the time.

Now and then the children of our Sunday School were expected to participate in the regular church service by reciting Biblical texts. When my class did so, our teacher, Miss Rendy Mason, wrote the texts on slips of paper and placed them like bookmarks in a hymnal. Then each of us drew one. The lucky drew short ones like "God is love" or, better still, "Jesus wept." These required only a spring across the platform and a mere glance at the congregation. Longer verses required a slower pace and longer exposure. So we hurried to count the words while Miss Rendy kept strict watch to be sure there was no trading.

On my Black Sunday I discovered, counting, that my verse had nine words in it. That alone was a disaster. I was upset at the start.

"For the Lord thy God," I read reluctantly, "is a jealous God."

The text was new to me, but not the word jealous. That was all too familiar, for I was a seventh child, submerged completely by my brothers and sisters. I loved them, but as I began to grow older their shadows hung perpetually over me. To their teachers (whose recollections were softened by time) they had all been models of brilliance, neatness, promptness, agreeableness, penmanship and deportment. Try as I did, I could never measure up. If I approached in one regard, I slipped badly in at least five others. Even my mother, who like other mothers of her time had never heard of sibling rivalry, often made comparisons. "Olive's neck is always clean," she would remind me. Or, "I can always count on John to remember." It was the same in the village. "You'll have to go some to catch up," one after another would tell me.

The weight of it would have been lightened had

people only called me by my own name. But few, except perhaps the neighbors, did. "Mornin' Edith," someone would greet me. Or "Bless my soul if it isn't Olive!" The postmaster, when he spoke to me at all, always prefaced any remark by asking, "Which one of the Chases are you?" I told him loudly, but it never registered. The next time he greeted me it would be by the name of one of my sisters. This troubled me greatly, for though I seldom had a letter of my own — valentines and such being delivered by hand — there always lurked in my mind the possibility that I might, and I feared somehow that I would never receive it. So being sent for the mail in the morning always gave me a bad start for the day.

When I sulked and refused to say what the matter was, my mother would talk solemnly to me about jealousy. It was, so it appeared, my Cardinal Sin. Yet it persisted, aggravated by the fact that things had to be done in turn in families. That wasn't so bad if you were a second or even a third child, but when you were a seventh it was another matter. Invariably the privilege you were to receive after interminable waiting turned out to be sadly depleted or at best to arrive at the wrong season. What especially stung was that, though it was my room as much as Olive's, I had the inside of the bed. *I* had the bottom drawers just because I was younger.

That Sunday, reading my verse, it all came to a head. I was jealous. God was jealous. Yet *I* was punished for something He could get away with. *I* was bad. Yet He was worshipped. He, who had no reason to be jealous at all. No one to boss Him. No models to live up to. He could be worshipped while *I* . . .

I felt myself nudged, then pushed. I do not know today what was going on within me. I only know that when I reached the platform, stumbling, I did not speak at all. I just stood there, frozen.

Miss Rendy began to prompt me in a whisper. "For the Lord . . . "

It had no effect.

She tried again, louder, her lips shaping the words. But I only stood there, unable or unwilling to speak. She tried still again, leaning almost out of the pew. This time she spoke aloud. I must have looked up, for I remember my mother's flushed face, saw her lips, too, moving. I saw the postmaster, the druggist, the dressmaker, neighbors, the butcher, the fishman, the grocer. The entire village, it seemed, all in a blur. Gradually their faces merged into one face, its mouth grimacing: "For the Lord, thy God . . . . " They knew He was jealous, yet they were all standing up for Him, taking His part. They knew He was as bad as I was. Still they expected me to praise His name. Well, I wouldn't, now or ever again. They couldn't make me.

What must have been two or three minutes passed with no sound but the loud tick of the clock and an undertone of hoarse whispers from the congregation. "For the Lord, thy God . . . " Then an impatient voice spoke. "Speak up, child," it said, "or God won't ever let you into Heaven."

That was too much for me. My rage boiled over. "If God's like that," I fairly shouted, "I wouldn't be in the same place with Him."

I closed my eyes and waited. Would He come as a lightning bolt through the ceiling and strike me dead? Or would the floor open and drop me straight into Hell? Or would the deacons rush forward and tear me limb from limb? Or would I, perhaps, like Lot's wife, be turned then and there into a pillar of salt?

But nothing whatever happened. Someone — I have never been sure who — came and led me to a seat in the wings where I sat rigid, staring at my patent leather shoes until the service was over. Then when all heads were bowed in the benediction, I raced quickly down a side aisle and through the swinging doors. Outside, I began to run, not down the road where the others would come, but toward the brook and the woods beyond where I sat on a boulder and waited. Let God get me there where no one could see.

When it became apparent that vengeance would be delayed, I got up and, walking very slowly, headed for home.

I opened the back door very quietly, intending to go upstairs. Normally I changed into my second-best dress and shoes when church was over. But that day I decided not to. I needed all the confidence my best clothes gave me. I would sit bolt upright in them and wait for what was coming. And I would sit on Olive's side of the bed.

Before I was halfway upstairs I heard my mother's voice. "We've been holding up dinner for you," she said.

Dinner was never held up for anyone except my father. I stood still, trying to take it in. Dinner waiting for me. For me, a sinner, who had expected no dinner at all . . .

"Hurry," she went on, raising her voice a little. "We're all ready to sit at the table."

I went cautiously into the dining room, eyes downcast, and slipped into my chair. Brothers and sisters, coached, as I was later to learn, said nothing.

I was always served last, as a matter of course. But that day when I started to pass on the first plate, my father spoke. "Keep it," he said. "It's yours."

Gratifying though that was, I still had the village to face, and the terror of confronting God himself had faded before the terror of going for the morning mail. I would be openly reproached, I told myself. Certainly shunned.

But it didn't happen that way at all. The druggist,

hurrying to open his store, patted me on the head with his paper as he passed. People who normally, if they saw me at all, greeted me with a half-wave or an automatic "Lo," smiled and said "Mornin." The doctor, coming down the steps of the post office, looked up from a letter he was reading and gave me what I was sure was a wink. But most astonishing of all was the behavior of the postmaster who, when he handed me the mail, actually called me by my own name.

Viva Victoria

hen I was born, my father had wanted
to call me Victoria, but my mother
would have none of it. "The child is
named already," she had said deci-
sively. This I was told at the age of six or seven by an
elderly aunt who at the same time warned me never to
bring the subject up. There had been, she confided with
a look of mystery, "quite a to-do" about it. Never good at
keeping secrets, I kept this one, for I valued my own name
then and wanted to run no chance of losing it.

My father was a Maine lawyer whose practice extended throughout the entire county. This necessitated a
good deal of travel, and to relieve the monotony of the
trips, made with horse and buggy, he often took one of
us children as a companion or, more accurately, an audience. He liked to think aloud, especially about his cases.
We enjoyed this if anything dramatic was involved. A barn
set on fire. Poison poured into a spring. An attack with a
hatchet. Less welcome were his renditions from famous

orations. An enthusiastic Anglophile, he was partial to the leading Parliamentarians, specializing in Pitt and Burke.

One day when I was about twelve, he interrupted a plea of Lord Melbourne and suddenly turned the horse off the main road and down a rutted, long-unused lane bordered by high cedars. "Let's take a look at Victoria's house," he said.

It was a name that, except as once mentioned by my aunt, I had never heard outside of the schoolroom. But I had not quite forgotten that there had been a "to-do," and now and then, signing my own name, had felt gratitude that my mother had won. Hearing the name now, so unexpectedly, embarrassed me a little. "Who is she, Papa?" I asked warily.

"An old lady," he answered. "She died before you were born. A most remarkable woman." There was a degree of respect in his voice that I had seldom heard.

In complete silence we bumped along the ruts and over the tufts of grasses. Soon we emerged from the shade of the cedars and drew up before an enormous yellow house ornamented with turrets and gables. There was an elegance about it which set it apart from the farmhouses we had passed, even from the most impressive houses in our village. The blinds were closed and peeling. Attached to the gate, now only a timbered frame, yet chained and locked, was a sign that read Balmoral.

The silence grew awkward. I began to wish that I had stayed at home. Finally I spoke. "Why would anyone give a house a name like that, Papa?" I asked timidly. To give a house a name at all was not customary in our parts.

"Because," he answered slowly, his eyes on the sign, "that was the name of the summer estate of Victoria, Queen of England." He turned the horse and we started home. He was quiet all the way.

Though baffled to know *why*, I felt that something all my fault had happened. I began to feel, too, that there were things my aunt had not revealed. But it was only some years after my father's death when I went through the papers in his office that, with help from my mother (her animosities now long forgotten), I was able to piece together the whole story.

Victoria had been my father's favorite client. This was not only because she paid her bills in cash (something rare indeed in the life of a country lawyer) but because he admired both individuality and tenaciousness in women. She had been born on the same day as the Queen herself, and this circumstance gave the two of them, she felt, a special bond. Her entire life had been devoted to the study and imitation of her royal counterpart.

Her posture was, of course, regal. She spoke with what she believed to be an English accent, but which, since she had never heard one, made her at times barely intelligible. She subscribed to all the major British periodicals; an expert seamstress, she faithfully copied the Queen's attire; an expert on genealogy, she knew the names, ages and exact relationship, including relationship by marriage, of at least four royal generations.

Founder and perpetual president of the Viva Victoria Society of America, she kept up an enormous correspondence with all its twenty-seven members, the nearest of whom was located in Columbus, Ohio. Moreover, she wrote an annual letter to the Queen on their mutual birthday. This alone took months of concentration. On the occasion of the Golden Jubilee she must have outdone herself, for she was rewarded almost two years later by a formal acknowledgement signed by a lady-in-waiting. This, framed, hung conspicuously on the wall near the foot of her bed where she could see it the first thing each morning. She always referred to it as "my correspondence with the Queen."

Above the fireplace in the sitting room was a pair of antlers placed exactly like those at Balmoral. These were flanked by two tartans, that of Albert and that of the Queen. On the mantel itself were framed portraits of all the royal family, cut from periodicals. The bookshelves held Scott's complete novels, favorites of the Queen, as well as books in German, which, when time allowed, she was determined to master.

Like the Queen, she was a widow and still, presumably, grieving. Her husband's portrait, delicately mustached and whiskered, hung in a dark corner of the dining room. His name (discordantly) was Hiram, a circumstance she must have found hard to bear. She was childless. When she lamented this, my mother had the feeling that her grief was less for the children she lacked than for the opportunity she had missed of presenting them with royal names. She did, however, have a dog which she kept constantly in her company. Like the Queen's dog, his name was Dash.

She kept a journal, underlined in the manner of the Queen's, with here and there a printed word or phrase. "Awakened at seven. Lay until *seven-thirty*. For breakfast OATMEAL, prunes, gooseberry tarts, *toasted muffin*. TWO cups of tea, *Green*. Re-read IN MEMORIAM. Here follows my reflections." Such reflections might run anywhere from three to twenty pages. (When she died, she had reached volume 82.)

Having, my mother insisted, worn out two other attorneys, she had selected my father, impressed by his knowledge of history, and she got great satisfaction out of their discussions, especially when they focused on the various Prime Ministers. Indeed, she regarded him as her own Prime Minister and took for granted his exclusive attention at any hour.

It was this more than anything else that had turned my mother against her. After Victoria became my father's client, nothing could be definitely planned, even on Sunday. The family might be getting ready for church or starting for an afternoon drive when a summons would come, borne by her hired man. Such a summons was always on a black-bordered card and signed simply Victoria. (The signature, perfected through years of tracing and plenty of practice, so closely resembled that of the Queen that even an experienced forger would have been impressed.) *Urgent. Expect you at four* such a message might read. Family plans for the day were over.

More aggravating still was her apparent assumption that she had a royal prerogative to change her mind. Two hours later, just as my father was about to start off, a fresh horse and an exhausted hired man might appear with another message, this one changing the time to six. No one else would have dared try my father's patience so far, least of all any of his own family.

But what annoyed my mother more was the arrival of an announcement that *he* could expect Victoria at such and such a time for dinner. My father had no comprehension of domestic affairs. "Just roast a piece of beef," he would say lightly, though the time of her arrival might be all but upon them. When she came, rarely at the hour she had set, a meal would somehow be ready. As she ate, gobbling in a way attributed to the Queen, she would ignore the rest of the family and engage my father in a discussion of some current parliamentary problem which she had read about in one of her British periodicals. "Quite a woman, Victoria," he would always observe, watching her drive off, erect and impressive in the back seat of her surrey.

I doubt that my mother would have been so forbearing but for one thing — Victoria's generosity. Victoria had only to hear through her housekeeper (she herself kept aloof from local affairs) of someone in need than she would notify my father to investigate and pay all costs. It might be only a matter of a grocer's bill or a cord of firewood. Or it might be considerably more. In one case it was to repair a house struck by lightning. In another it was to forestall a foreclosure. When my father reminded her that her own funds were limited, she would brush his words aside. "It's only what the Queen does every day," she told him.

When it was time to draw up her will, she announced to my father that she wished to leave her money for a statue of the Queen. He attempted to convince her that there would be too many difficulties involved. But she was unmoved. She had, she assured him, full confidence in his ability to handle anything. What really concerned him was her financial situation. Depleted by gifts, her principal would little more than see her through.

"There'll be hundreds of statues of the Queen," he argued. "All over the empire. One more wouldn't be noticed at all." He bent to pat Dash, lying at her feet. "Everything for the Queen," he said soberly, "and nothing for Dash. The Queen wouldn't want him forgotten. Why don't you leave what's left to the County Shelter for Animals? On condition that they change its name," he added quickly.

She looked interested but not convinced.

The next day he wrote up such a will and took it over to her. She read it with interest, but he could not persuade her to sign. "The Queen is well," she said serenely. It was her firm conviction that, their lives having been, as she saw it, so closely interwoven, they would die on the same day.

Late in December of 1900 the papers began carrying rumors of the Queen's ill health. Victoria's appetite left her. She no longer had strength, she complained, to write in her journal. By the end of the month she came down with a heavy cold. She wouldn't hear of having the doctor, but she did take to her bed, concerned only with arrival of the Boston papers. At the first of the year the house-keeper took matters into her own hands. That night the doctor called my father.

"It's pneumonia," he said. "She hasn't a chance."

My father started at once for Balmoral.

"What of the Queen?" she whispered as he entered the room. "Is she living still?"

He went over to the bed and placed his hand over hers. "At the moment," he told her choosing his words with care. Then he took the will from his pocket, placed Dash closer to her, and handed her a pen.

She signed.

As the days passed, she became more feeble. Her pulse weakened. She slept very little.

The doctor was puzzled. "I wish I knew what's keeping her alive," he said.

My father knew.

By the middle of the month it was obvious that she could breathe only with great pain. When she could no longer speak, her eyes asked the same question. "What of the Queen?"

On the twenty-second my father could bear her suffering no longer. "Victoria," he shouted. He always shouted when he was about to tell a lie. "I've just called Boston. The Queen is dead."

She stared, gave a long sigh of relief, closed her eyes, and almost at once stopped breathing.

The next day the Boston papers made his words official. Queen and commoner had died together.

78

In this conformist world in which we live, painfully seeking an identity, I often think with admiration and a little envy of Victoria and wish that I had been given her name.

Les Chapeaux

iss Emma Osgood was the telephone operator in our little Maine village. The switchboard was in her dining room where, under ordinary circumstances, the sideboard would have been. Because of the infrequency of calls (the village had exactly twenty-two phones), she had another occupation. She was the village milliner.

She did not sell hats. There would have been no profit in it, for a hat in our village was a family possession to be passed on from one member to another. She merely trimmed hats. Since she was creative by nature, she preferred her needle to her earphones, and frequent complaints were made, always out of her hearing, that the red light on her switchboard often flashed unnoticed while she deliberated between a quill and a cherry.

Miss Emma's fees were extremely reasonable. For thirty-five cents (twenty-five for the ornament and ten cents for the know-how) she would transform any aged hat into a fresh creation. A dip here, secured by a tight bunch of forget-me-nots; a fold somewhere else, backed up with a daisy; a strip of velvet across the crown; a new piece of elastic — and there you were! If you wanted to economize, you could supply your own material — a bit of lace, perhaps, from a discarded fichu or a feather from your own rooster.

However, versatile as she was, Miss Emma found me something of a problem. I was the fifth girl in my family. By the time a hat reached me, it was almost beyond disguise. Miss Emma would ponder, frowning, trying first one thing then another until some child sent by an exasperated parent would dash in, call her attention to the flashing switchboard, and inform her that the call was urgent.

The call put through, she would return, sighing, to her problem. Unfortunately, my mother's taste ran to sailor hats. Now there is just so much you can do to these, and when one reached Miss Emma for the fourth time, she clearly felt that my mother was expecting the impossible. Watching her aggrieved face as she turned and fingered, I made a resolution. Some day I would buy myself a hat in Paris. That was the beginning of this story.

I did not to go to Paris until 1952 when I was what Miss Emma would have called a woman grown. I had had many hats between this time and the time I had sat by her switchboard, most of them reasonably becoming, though none of them — let me hasten to add — a sailor. But the dream of a Paris hat still persisted.

Our trip was a short one. Its climax was Paris. We were to spend three days there; then my husband was to fly back home. I was to follow the next day by boat with the luggage.

"You can buy some books and prints after I leave," my husband had told me in making our plans. I had nodded guiltily. Normally I should have liked nothing better than to buy some books and prints. But not that day. On that day I was going to buy a hat — that hat I'd felt I had coming to me all my life.

During lunch on the day of my husband's departure we counted our money soberly. We had spent a great deal more than we had expected to. There had been an outrageous dental bill in Switzerland; in Germany there had been an accident to our rented car. "I can leave you around forty dollars," he said. "I don't feel right about it, but I guess you can manage. Your hotel bill will be paid. This should take care of your meals and your taxi."

And a hat besides, I thought doggedly.

I had no idea how much a hat would cost in Paris. I had heard stories of some that had cost fifty dollars, some that had cost one hundred dollars. But I had expected that in some little shop, away from the fashionable district, I might possibly get one for twenty-five dollars. That would still leave me fifteen dollars. With a Paris hat on my head, food would be irrelevant.

I went with him to the field. As soon as his plane was called, he passed me a handful of francs. "Here is a note for 10,000 francs. That is twenty-eight dollars, remember," he said. "And here are four notes for 1000. Now if anything happens . . . "

"I can take care of myself," I told him confidently.

As soon as his plane was off the ground I got into a taxi and headed back toward our hotel, a modest one on the Left Bank, near Luxembourg Gardens. We had chosen it because it was inexpensive and because we had been told that tourists seldom went there. The concierge spoke English, but no one else did, nor did anyone in the neighboring shops.

In the window of one of these shops, directly across from the hotel, I had seen a smart black beret. If it looked well on me and cost no more than twenty-five dollars, I had determined that I would buy it. As we approached the shop, I called out to the driver, *"Arrêtez-vous, s'il vous plaît."* It was the only French phrase I could speak with authority.

We stopped. I jumped out. My eyes on the window, I hurriedly pulled a note from my purse and gave it to the driver. He sped away, beaming. When he was out of sight, I discovered that instead of a thousand-franc note as I had intended, I had given him the note for ten thousand.

A bench was directly across the street under a chestnut tree and, weak with dismay, I sank down upon it. I now had roughly twelve dollars. It would feed me and get me and my luggage to the boat. There might even be a few dollars left over. But the hat, of course, was out of the question.

I got up dejectedly and started for the hotel. But I could not pass the black beret without a glance. Pert and tailored, it was made of crisp, lustrous faille — the kind of hat you could wear with anything, in any season. A truly sophisticated hat. One that would unfailingly draw eyes.

My glance grew prolonged. This was not a conventional beret, for it was high in the back and its slant came forward. On the padded stick that held it, it seemed to lift, almost to fly. What might it not do to a face? I thought. A face well past forty. But for my stupidity, what might it not have done to mine?

As I stood there, the proprietor came to the door. She was a bird-like woman with a big chest, tiny legs, and very bright eyes. I had often seen her standing on her topmost step as if ready for flight. Occasionally she had smiled as I came out of the hotel, and once or twice we had exchanged a pleasant *"Bonjour."* She smiled at me now as if I were an old friend.

"Aimez-vous le petit béret?" she asked.

"*Oui, oui, Madame,*" I answered.

She look gratified. Then she held out one of her small hands, ringed on almost every finger. "*Entrez, Madame,*" she said. Had her manner been insistent, I would have backed away. But it was not. It was as though our mutual admiration of the black beret had somehow tightened a bond that already existed between us. "*Entrez,*" she said again.

What harm could it do? At least I would have the satisfaction of knowing how I would look in a Paris hat.

I went inside. It was a tiny shop — a bird's nest, really. In the center was a table on which a dozen hats were gathered. Following Madame's gesture, I sat down in a little gilt chair before a large gilt mirror while she delicately picked up the black beret and reverently placed it on my head. Looking at myself, I forgot every sailor hat I had ever worn. If only Miss Emma could see me now, I thought.

Madame appeared as impressed as I was. "*C'est fait pour vous. Pour vous,*" she cried, clasping her jeweled fingers.

A little alarmed, I shook my head firmly. Still there was no denying that it was becoming — that it was, in fact, *the* hat for me. I cursed my carelessness.

"*Mais oui! Mais oui!*" she cried, twisting her hands with visible distress.

Could I have spoken her language or she have comprehended mine, I would have told her the whole story, and she would, I felt sure, have understood and sympathized. But my French vocabulary was almost exhausted. I looked carefully around the room. There were blue hats, pink hats, brown hats. There was no other beret.

"*Je ne cherche pas un béret noir,*" I said laboriously. "*Je cherche un béret vert.*"

"*Un béret vert?*" She looked thoughtful.

Fearful there might have been a green one I had overlooked, I added quickly, *"Je cherche aussi un béret blanc."* In this way, so it seemed to me, I had kept myself free from any possible commitment.

"Un béret vert? Un béret blanc?" she repeated.

I nodded. Then feeling both secure and linguistically eloquent, I turned for one last look at myself in the mirror. It was a long look. While it was going on, Madame raised her voice and spoke in rapid French. I did not even try to follow her words. I was too intent on fixing in my mind the picture of myself, smart, svelte, lifted. . . .

A customer came in, and Madame left me undisturbed. I looked at myself full-faced. I picked up a mirror and admired both profiles. I examined myself chin raised, then lowered. I tipped the hat a little forward. I moved it back again. I tried the effect while wearing my glasses. It was still striking. While Madame and her customer became engrossed in a brown velour, I assumed subdued poses. I nodded modestly as though meeting a less well-dressed acquaintance. I listened intently as if at a lecture.

It seemed to me no time at all before a door at the rear of the shop burst open, and a man entered with daring motions and a smile that flashed and faded like the light on Miss Emma's switchboard. Smaller even than Madame, he was wearing a faded smock, and around his neck on a long cord hung a pair of enormous shears. In one hand he was extending something green and bulky, in the other something white.

Staring, I saw that they were embryonic berets. Horror hit me. Alone in Paris, without money enough to buy one hat, I had unwittingly ordered two, both custom-made.

I knew I must do something. Yet at the same time I realized there was nothing I could do. The hats were cut and formed already.

Madame picked up a pin cushion and rushed to my

side. The little man, his great shears knocking against his knees, removed the black beret from my head and put the green one in its place.

I closed my eyes. The only thing I could do was to wire for money. How much would they cost? At least a hundred dollars, I decided. In 1952 that amount was a good deal of money in anybody's family. It bought groceries for a month. Fillings for twenty cavities. Three pairs of glasses. . . . I had done this. I, who could take care of myself. I, the practical, sensible wife. I, the unselfish mother. I sagged in my chair, and solicitously the shears grew silent.

"*Etes-vous fatiguée, Madame?*"

"*Non, non,*" I said, and tried to straighten.

But could I be sure the hats would cost only a hundred dollars? One custom-made hat I had heard of had cost two hundred and fifty dollars, and no one had ever seen anything special about it. My palms became damp. I felt a dull humming in my ears. I swayed with the placing of each pin. Vaguely, far off, I could head Madame's ecstatic twittering.

Finally it was over. "*Regardez!*" Madame cried. "*Regardez!*"

I opened my eyes and looked. A shocked, pale face with a tinge of the faille itself looked back at me. That was all I saw. I did not look above it.

"*Ah, que c'est beau! Ravissant!*" the little man exclaimed, flashing his smile.

I smiled back weakly. Then I closed my eyes again. I felt one hat removed and another replace it. But I felt nothing else. Instead of diminishing, my state of shock had grown. Madame had to shake me by the shoulder when the little man was done. When I opened my eyes, she was standing beside me, a calendar in her hand. She lifted the top leaf and pointed to the one beneath it.

Dully I understood. She meant that the hats would be ready for me the next day. Again she pointed, this time in quick succession to the hats, herself, and then to my hotel. Again I understood. She herself would deliver them.

I nodded, rose, and went outside. It was nearly six o'clock and the street was crowded. Dazed, I worked my way across it and to a sidewalk cafe, intending to buy a cup of coffee. But before I could sit down I caught myself. I must not spend a single franc.

Back in the hotel I lay on the bed and started to compose the wire to my husband. Should I say: NEED MONEY FOR PURCHASES? No, I told myself. That was too matter-of-fact. I must, I felt, convey something of my distress. Should I say: NEED MONEY FOR EMERGENCY? No. That would scare him. He would send all the money we had, and it took money to send money. He might even fly back. Should I say: NEED MONEY FOR DEBTS?

How much did I need? I realized suddenly that I did not know. In leaving I had been too stunned to ask the price. I got up, hurried downstairs, and crossed the street, but the shop was closed. I shook the latch without response. I peeked through the window. The nest was empty.

Madame was at dinner, I thought. I felt hungry myself. At the pastry shop on the corner I bought two hard rolls and took them to the Luxembourg Gardens. There, militantly protecting myself from the pigeons, I ate them soberly.

I was not worried about getting the money. My husband's plane would arrive at seven. He would be home by nine. He would send a wire by ten. I should get it by noon, or by one o'clock at the latest. The boat train did not leave until three. It seemed a safe margin. What depressed me was my own stupidity. Why had I entered the shop in the first place?

At eight-thirty I went back to the shop again. It was still closed. All up and down the street other shops were closing. On the bench under the chestnut I waited another hour. Then I went to the corner to send my wire. NEED MONEY, I wrote. NOW.

Back in the hotel I went at once to bed. For hours I lay awake, seething with self-recrimination. I would never wear the hats, I told myself. I might not even take them with me. The streets were quiet before I slept.

At dawn I woke suddenly. Ten a.m. was three p.m. in Paris, I remembered. The money would start just as the boat train was leaving. I jumped out of bed and began to pack my bags. I would not wait for the boat train. I would run away. I would leave Paris. I would take the very next train to Cherbourg and wait on the dock. When Madame came, she would not find me.

But before my bags were half-packed, my New England conscience had caught up with me. I had ordered those hats, albeit in ignorance. I was responsible for paying for them. Shivering, I went back to bed. Things were now out of my hands. I would tell the concierge the whole story. He would call the police, and I would throw myself upon their mercy.

At exactly quarter to nine the next morning my telephone rang. "*Les chapeaux, Madame,*" the desk clerk said.

"*Merci,*" I answered.

I was calmer now, for I had worked out a plan. Madame obviously loved jewelry. I would offer her my pearl necklace and earrings, my watch, as well as all my remaining money, saving out only my taxi fare to the boat train. If that was not enough, I would propose my engagement ring as security (this, however, only to the police).

In the lobby Madame stood waving both arms, like

wings, as she watched the lift descend. In each hand was a bouncing, bright-pink hatbox. *"Bonjour, Madame,"* she called.

"Bonjour," I echoed faintly.

Beaming, she drew me to the lounge and archly opened first one box and then the other, revealing the finished berets. Depressed as I was, I could not help but start with pleasure. All the qualities of the black beret were there in both of them — its lilt, its zest, its smartness.

"Combien?" I asked hoarsely.

Madame pursed her lips and thought a moment. *"Vingt-quatre cents francs,"* she finally said.

"Vingt-quatre cents francs," I whispered after her. At the same time I ran my finger down the little chart I always carried. Twenty-four hundred francs was only six dollars and eighty-six cents. It could not be.

Thinking I had not understood, Madame took a pad and pencil from her commodious purse. *2400 francs*, she wrote. I stared at the figures. I closed my eyes and stared again. It was too good to be true. Then the two hats together would be less than fourteen dollars. I had eight dollars left after having paid for the wire and saved out the money for my taxi. I would owe Madame only six. I turned to look for the concierge. He was not in sight. I decided to try sign language.

I took the eight dollars — exactly 2800 francs — from my purse and gave them to Madame. She sat down and began to count them. While she was doing this, I took off my necklace and earrings. They were worth at least ten dollars. I could keep my watch and my engagement ring. If I could only convince Madame. . . .

I laid the jewelry on the table. Before I could speak Madame got up and extended her hand. It held four hundred francs. I was thrown completely. "I do not know," I said. *"Je ne comprehend pas."*

Madame gave me a patient look. She placed one hat box on top of the other and raised two fingers. *"Vingt-quatre cents francs,"* she said, *"pour les deux."*

This happened, as I have said, in 1952. I lost the white beret the next year during a visit to my little Maine village. It blew off, oddly enough, in front of the house that had once held Miss Emma's switchboard. I was so struck by the coincidence that I made no attempt to retrieve it until it was damaged beyond repair. But I still wear the green one, and it never fails to evoke comment.

"Such a stunning hat," someone is sure to say. "And so unusual. I've never seen another like it."

I drop my eyes modestly. "It's custom-made," I answer. "I had it done in Paris."

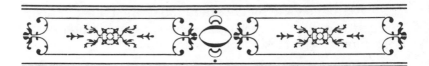

Attention: Saint Patrick

ooking back, it seems ridiculous that I had not suspected something sooner. I had bought the place — a sturdy, story-and-a-half Maine farmhouse, furnished, together with fifty acres bordering the salt water — for three thousand dollars from a man who had left in a highly nervous state. Though there were a great many rat holes about — in fact, a perfect commutation system between attic and cellar — I had seen no signs of rats or mice during the four weeks I had lived alone there. To be sure, I had heard them, though less and less frequently, in the walls at night. I had heard other sounds, too, sounds which reflection might have told me had been footless and gliding. But the fact was I had been too busy for reflection.

Built in 1776, the house had never been modernized. Lamps had to be cleaned and filled, kindling chopped. Wood and drinking water had to be carried. The cookstove was a hazard, for with no perceptible provocation the door of the firebox would spring suddenly open, spewing sparks and embers. This meant it could never be left alone while in action. (Indeed, for real security, you had to sit alert and ready on the woodbox, a pail of water within quick reach.) Between chores, there was wallpaper to peel and paint to spread. Then, of course, there were letters to write — swaggering, ebullient letters full of romantic detail (especially about the attic and its old trunks, crammed with ancient documents); letters full, too, of reckless hospitality. So, all in all, I had had no time to dream up trouble.

The house had only one real bedroom, and that was downstairs, off the kitchen. But the attic had been divided into two unfinished rooms, and because I like the sound of rain on the roof, I slept in one of them. Then one morning I woke and saw on the floor, not three feet from my bed, two long, freshly discarded snake skins.

Now I am not a brave woman. My staying alone had been only from pride and bravado. I had bought the place without any investigation. Indeed, I had bought it by telephone without even having seen the interior. Then I had simply moved in, shutting my eyes to any possible complications. Now my family was waiting smugly for my flight. So were the villagers. Every day they drove by looking, not without some anticipation, for evidence of disaster. For an entire month I had astonished everyone. But could I stay on, living with snakes?

These were no mere garter snakes, the skins had told me. These were milk snakes, not poisonous, to be sure, but repulsive creatures: thick, sluggish, and covered with blotches. I knew them from my childhood. They often got in cellars, I remembered, through bulkheads left open or through loosened screens. But these, bolder, had obviously come up through the walls to the second story and, finding plenty of mice to feed on, stayed.

Except for one thing I might have forgotten my pride and fled the place forever. My first guest Beth Williams, was to arrive in two days from Cleveland. While I had a few friends to whom I might have confided my plight, Beth was definitely not one of them. We had taken biology together in college — that is, we had taken it together until Beth got her first close-up of an earthworm, when she had turned a strange color (chartreuse, one observer described it) and dropped the course. By now she had already left Cleveland. No trumped-up tale could reach and stop her. Somehow I must get rid of the snakes before she came.

I could, I told myself, use poison, but if I did they might die in the walls; or, reasonably, since they had shed their skins there, on the floor by my bed. Then I would have to carry them off, limp and heavy, for burial.

No, I decided, there must be an easier way, a way of getting rid of them without ever having to see them, dead or alive. But how could I find out? Impulsively I thought of asking a neighbor, but almost at once decided against it. Then I thought of the village library. I would go there, find a book on the habits of snakes and handle the matter scientifically.

Leaving the skins where they were, I tiptoed unsteadily downstairs and started off. All the way, one thought possessed me. There had been two snakes, obviously adult and healthy. How long might it be before there were more? How many should one expect from a serpentine accouchement? Where did such a thing take place? In a bureau drawer, or perhaps, more snugly, in a bed?

Since the library had never been catalogued, I was obliged to ask for what I wanted. "I should like to see a book on snakes," I said, trying to assume the air of a naturalist.

The librarian searched the shelves. Finally she turned, her finger on a narrow volume. "I can't find a thing about snakes," she said. "Wouldn't you just as soon have butterflies?"

"Gladly," I said with some fervor. "The only thing is, I *have* snakes."

She backed away from me.

"I thought I might find a book that told me how to get rid of them," I hurried to say.

"Well," she said, still edging off, "I'll look among the books that never go out."

In a few minutes she came back extending at arm's length a book called *Snakes: Their Whys and Hows.*

Feeling some hope, I turned at once to the Hows. *How To Identify Snakes . . . How To Feed Them . . . How To Raise Them . . . How To Make Them Into Pets . . .* These were definitely not my chapters. I read on. But there was no chapter called *How To Get Them Out Of An Attic.* Indeed, a quick perusal of an earlier chapter *Where They Live* made no mention of their frequenting attics at all.

But I did learn something pertinent to my predicament. A snake, I read, having shed its skin, suffers temporarily from a weakened memory. This was disconcerting. A normal snake, forewarned of my approach, would, I had figured, be smart enough to get out of the way. But what about a snake with a weakened memory? Would he be likely to wander about so that I might come upon him almost anywhere — dozing perhaps on a pillow or cuddled deep in a rubber boot? How would he act if apprehended?

A later chapter answered that question. "Each species," I read, "has its own threatening pose which serves as a background for still more alarming hissing, spreadings, inflating, opening of the mouth or even striking."

No, I decided, pride or no pride, I would never go into that house again.

But there was Beth coming. . . .

95

Desperately I read on, and it was not long before I found a ray of hope. All snakes, it seemed, though unable to hear, were sensitive to vibration. Why not use that to drive them out? I had two days.

I hurried home, took the hoe from the shed against any emergency, and opened the back door. Inside, I stamped, rattled the covers of the stove, kicked the wood-box, and pounded the ceilings with my hoe. Then I went to the stairway, opened the door, looked cautiously in all directions, and, still carrying my hoe; clumped heavily upward. With a faint, unreasonable surprise, I saw that the skins lay just as I had found them. Poking them with my hoe, I got them on a piece of paper, rolled them up and, shuddering, took them outside. Then I went upstairs again, seized my night clothes and hurried back down. I could sleep in the little bedroom off the kitchen until Beth came. During her visit I would spend the night on the horsehair settee in the parlor.

During the next two days I intensified my vibrations. I banged doors, I worked the pump until the screws fell out of it, I pounded the floor while the firebox fell open and the covers of the cookstove rattled. At regular intervals I marched from room to room drumming the dishpan like a witch doctor, and uttering loud incantations. No snake, I figured, not even a snake with a blunted memory, would put up with a hullabaloo like that for long.

Beth came in the late afternoon. Her interest in the view was perfunctory, in the rooms downstairs, only po-lite. "It's the attic I want to see," she told me. "Your letters made it sound absolutely fascinating. I can hardly wait to get at those trunks. Can't we begin right now?"

She had caught me unprepared. "It's getting dark," I said, considerably shaken. "You'll notice that it gets dark very early here."

96

"Couldn't we take a lamp up with us?" she asked.

"A lamp's dangerous, Beth," I said, floundering, "with all that stuff around."

She looked disappointed. "Well, in the morning then," she said. "Very early."

Here was a new worry. How could I stop her? If she started moving trunks around, what might she find? Why had I written those letters, anyway?

Seated in the parlor, we did not talk much. I played a few college songs rather halfheartedly on the old organ and then suggested that we go to bed. I could see that the dark and the silence were having an intimidating effect on Beth.

"Where do you sleep?" she asked.

"In the attic," I lied. I would putter around until she was sound asleep. Then I would cramp up on the old settee, ache out the night, and get up ahead of her in the morning. For all she would know, I had slept upstairs. "But I'm not going yet," I said. "I have some things to tend to. You go ahead."

"No," she said firmly. "I'll go when you do."

I brought in enough wood to last out a blizzard and dropped it noisily in the box. I banged each door before I locked it. I took out the screens and let the windows fall. Then, since she was still there, waiting, I could do nothing but pick up my flashlight and start upstairs.

"Good night," I said, trying to sound casual. In a few minutes she would drop off; then I could creep down and into the parlor.

Upstairs I gingerly removed each piece of bedding and shook it. Then I lay down, fully clothed, clutching the hoe.

Half an hour passed. I could hear Beth still stirring. But there had been no other sounds. An hour passed. There was complete silence. I began to relax. The vibrations had worked, I told myself. The snakes had left me. I thought of the hard, cold, slippery settee and decided to stay where I was. I laid the hoe quietly on the floor and pulled up the blanket.

Just about dawn I woke suddenly, hearing a sound like heavy breathing. Softly in . . . Heavily out . . . In . . . Out . . . It came from the stairs.

No one was there. No one could be. They were low stairs, and I could see half way down them without lifting my head. I was just having some kind of nervous reaction. Then I heard it again. In . . . Out. . . .

Beth heard it, too. "Where are you?" she called sharply.

The sound stopped suddenly.

"I'm here," I said in a feeble voice. "In the attic."

"Didn't I hear you on the stairs?"

"No, no, you're dreaming."

For a few minutes there was silence. Though I was drenched with sweat, I dared not move to throw my blanket back. Then I heard a new sound, not from the stairs but from the floor beside me — not a sound like breathing this time, but a gentle crackle. I turned my head stiffly. Dim though it was, the light from the window showed me, dark against some old papers I had strewn about, a thick, twisting line moving sluggishly toward the stairs.

Quick, my brain told me. You can get it with the hoe.

But not a muscle moved.

Then I heard the other sound again.

In . . . Out . . . In . . . Out. . . .

Both snakes were on the stairs.

Never in my wildest apprehensions had I dreamed that such a thing might happen. Snakes might ascend and descend within walls, twisting their way among laths and plaster. This I granted. They did, obviously, traverse attic floors. But descending stairs. . . .

Get them, my brain prompted. You know where they are. Get them now. But I lay rigid.

What if I didn't get them? What if Beth, hearing the commotion, came running? The snakes, caught between us, would surely get emotional. I thought of them there in the dark, puffing and hissing and inflating and all the other things the book had told about. Then I thought of Beth, turning chartreuse in the kitchen. . . .

I tried to get hold of myself. There was nothing to be upset about. The snakes were simply going outside. They had to have water. I ought to have remembered that. Quite naturally, now that I came to think of it, they would prefer stairs to walls for descent. Perhaps they hesitate on every stair. But I did figure out their route. They would go by way of the rat-holes to the cellar, then out through the chinks in the foundation.

Suddenly horror seized me. They couldn't go to the cellar. In dressing up the house for Beth's inspection, I had placed a flatiron tight against the rat-hole in the door leading to the cellar.

I began to shiver.

Where are they now? Suppose, denied their exit, they should go in Beth's room and vent their frustration there?

There was only one thing to do, and I had to do it. I got up, still shivering, grabbed the hoe with one hand and the flashlight with the other, and started downstairs. Stair by stair I went, then step by step into the quiet, shadowy kitchen. First I tiptoed to Beth's door. She was sleeping soundly. I ran the flashlight over her floor, but except for her shoes and slippers it was bare. I closed the door and opened wide the cellar door in the kitchen. Then, circling my flashlight so that nothing could creep up unseen behind me, I began my search.

First I went systematicallly over every visible inch of the floor. Nothing. Next I approached the stove and examined all its crevices. Nothing. Then, my flashlight wavering in my hand, I went to the woodbox and took out every stick. Nothing stirred.

I went to the icebox, bent, and gingerly drew out the pan. Then, crouching, I took the hoe and ran its handle underneath.

Just at that moment, in a position from which I was entirely helpless to attack or defend, I heard a stir from the direction of the sink — a clink of basins, followed by a brisk, smooth scuttle.

Then I heard the familiar sound, this time more rapid.

In . . . Out. . . .

It came from the cellar stairs. Well, one snake was gone . . . Where was the other?

I got up shakily. The dawn, growing, touched the mirror above the table and showed me my face. I looked a little chartreuse myself.

While I stood, trying to collect myself, I heard a sound from the dining room.

For an instant I thought I must give up, wake Beth, and flee with her. Then I remembered the neighbors and got myself in hand.

Between the kitchen and the dining room was a narrow hall that led outside. I went through it and opened the outer door. Then I crossed the dining room and closed the door which led from it into the front hall. Being nervous, I did this hurriedly, neglecting to fasten the latch. Instead of working as I should have, like a beater, from the outer edges, closing in, I began near the corner closet. While I was searching that, I heard a movement on the hearth. It was dawn now, and turning, I saw the snake dart sleekly through the hall door, which had swung open, toward the parlor, leaving a thin, diminishing line of ashes.

By the time I had reached the parlor, stopping on the way to latch the dining room door and open the front one, the snake had disappeared. So had my fear. These snakes were cowardly creatures. Obviously they had no yen to hiss or bloat. Moreover, they were outsmarting me.

From then on, I meant business. Profiting by experience, I began in the farthest corner where the organ stood and worked left toward the open front door. I worked aggressively now. I pulled the books from the bookcase. I overturned the magazine bucket. I stirred the ashes in the fireplace.

Nothing.

I began with the organ again and worked to the right. I yanked the cushions from the settee, pulled some cattails from a jardiniere, and peered inside. I even opened the drawer of the table. Nothing.

There was only one other possible place, I told myself. That was behind the organ.

Approaching from the left, I stopped about two feet off and knocked it with my hoe, expecting the snake to escape from the right, which was the direction of the door.

Nothing happened.

I went closer and shook the organ with both hands.

I leaned over the top, and saw nothing.

The organ was on casters. Crouching, I poked about with the handle of the hoe. I felt nothing.

I stood erect and listened.

In a minute or two I heard a click from the inner recesses of the organ.

So there you are, I thought.

102

I poked the handle of the hoe over first one pedal, then the other. Nothing moved. I tried again more vehemently, but with no more success.

Then I sat dejectedly on the organ stool, watching the east. In a little while it would be morning. I could not leave the snake there to come out at will. Yet if I moved the organ and really went after it, Beth would hear and come running just in time to see the chase. That must never happen.

Suddenly I had an inspiration. I seized the braided rug that lay before the organ and flung it over the pedals. Then I sat down on the stool again, pulled out all the stops, pressed hard against the knee swells, and pumped with all my strength. At the same time with both hands I hit the lowest keys. They responded with thunderous vibration.

On the very first chord the snake shot out, crossed the room with hardly an undulation, and disappeared through the front door.

I continued to play on with great chords of triumph until Beth, in her nightgown, opened the parlor door.

"What is it?" she demanded. "What's happening around here?"

I looked up innocently. "Why, nothing," I said. "Nothing at all. You said you wanted to get up early. Remember?"

Do I Hear Five?

here is nothing I would rather do than go to an auction. As soon as the notice of one appears in the county paper, my blood starts stirring. Fatigue disappears. Poison ivy stops itching. Blisters suddenly heal. Though I cannot weed a garden for ten minutes at midday without dizziness, even collapse, I can stay for hours under the blazing sun in some farmyard listening to the compelling voice of a Maine auctioneer.

My family, alas, feels less enthusiasm. While I am making the sandwiches, slapping on the peanut butter, they delay over breakfast, making pointed remarks about the crowded state of our attic and the depleted state of our finances. Dressing, they debate among themselves whether it is better to sit with me and suffer mortification (I being an audible bidder and prone to raise questions) or to sit apart, preserving their dignity, yet leaving me unrestrained.

But when we are about five miles from the site, they,

too, catch something of the fever, for the roads are crowded with farm trucks, station wagons, convertibles, even a motorcycle or two, all headed in the same direction. Though (due entirely to my own initiative) we are always early, we can never park as close as we want to, for, fully a quarter of a mile from the white flag, cars have been left everywhere, even in the ditches.

We fit in where we can and push our way forward, jostling picnic baskets, knitting bags, baby strollers, camp chairs, umbrellas. Women are always in the lead. Perhaps the men are remembering the sideboards or the marble-topped commodes tried out in every room in the house and finally stored away in the barn chamber.

When we get there what a jumble lies before us! Cut glass. Blown glass. Pressed glass. Milk glass. Sandwich. Hobnail. China dishes, their patterns half obscured by grime. Books with swollen pages and faded loosened covers. Teapots with chipped or broken noses. A coffee grinder that someone will grab for a lamp base. A bird cage that will ultimately support ivy. A splendid pair of Bristol vases . . .

Felt hats, straw hats, hats with broken, dusty feathers. Sad irons and vinegar jugs by the dozen. One or two conch shells. A heap of shoes with laces that no one could ever untangle. Old clocks, a few still running. Old quilts. A box of patent medicines. A Sheffield silver platter . . .

Chairs in rows and heaps. Caned bottom, slat bottom, bottomless altogether. Chairs upholstered in plush or horsehair. Chairs with broken rungs and springs protruding. A rosewood Salem rocker. Kitchen tables, scarred by knives and marked by hot dishes. Parlor tables, their veneer warped and peeling. A Chippendale tilt-top table that will send the bids soaring.

105

Dressers with stubborn drawers and missing handles. Commodes, always pungent. Spool beds, four posters. Braided rugs and musty carpets. Kitchen ranges. Farm tools. Harnesses. Andirons. Lanterns. Hanging lamps with prisms missing, and tangled rusty chains. Mirrors tarnished and mottled. Sea chests with rope beckets, still smelling faintly of tar . . . A hooded cradle . . .

We look them all over, then we set up our camp stools and inspect the crowd. Sharp-eyed dealers, near the front, of course, where they can spot a piece of cranberry glass or Staffordshire. Farm wives, brown-skinned and hearty, thankful to be sitting. Tourists all agog at finding local color. Children everywhere, already demanding root beer or Coca-Cola. Villagers, like ourselves, who leave the halters and the shorts to the tourists and the summer people. Husbands on the outskirts, looking on with careful nonchalance.

Right on schedule the proceedings start. The teller, all business, takes her cashbox to her table. Then the auctioneer appears, ready to make a day of it. He shakes a few select hands, thus conferring status, makes some general remarks, concluding with a joke or two, picks up a jug or a firkin, maybe, and begins.

"Well, folks, what am I offered?"

A good Maine auctioneer is a match for any psychologist living. Each has his own special technique, his own brand of persuasion. Some use the question method. *Five. May I have six? May I have seven?* Some use coaxing. *The dollar and the quarter. Now the dollar and the half.* Some are imperative. *Five make it six. Six. Make it seven.* Some use gestures, snatching out the bids, as it were, turning from one bidder to another with such mounting speed that they are both caught in a rhythm they are reluctant, sometimes unable, to break. Some auctioneers encourage verbal bids, believing that they engender en-

107

thusiasm. Some prefer a raised hand or merely a nod in confirmation. (After all, it is easier to nod fifteen dollars than to say it.) Dealers are seldom verbal. The auctioneer knows them all, and a raised finger on an unraised hand is enough.

"A quarter I have. Now the thirty-five."

"Thirty-five," someone calls and the thing is his at a bargain. For the first thing up is a gimmick every time.

Then the real bidding begins. There is no telling at the start how it will go. The weather has a lot to do with it. On a hot day the crowd, plagued by heat and sunburn, is often more concerned with cold drinks than with china. On a rainy day people are too busy jostling for a dry place to stand to get worked up over a rabbit-eared chair or an Empire table, though a bottle of furniture polish may be offered as a lure. In wind, behavior is erratic. Likely as not no one will offer a dime for a spool bedstead, but a hat-rack started at fifty cents will rise suddenly to seven or eight dollars. A compote, publicly returned because of a crack, will sell a second time for twice as much as before.

The ideal day is cool and dry. The auctioneer shakes more hands than usual. The crowd is good-humored and sociable. Faces seen at other auctions become the faces of friends. Greetings, sometimes confidences, are exchanged. Tips are passed on to known collectors. *Round Pond is the place for ironstone.* Or *Go to Gardiner if you want clocks.* Even the dealers are affable.

"Well, folks, what am I offered?"

Coal scuttles. Picture frames. Boxes of buttons. Beaded lamp shades. Family albums. A coil of rope. A Lazy Susan. A milk stool. A pewter teapot. Old guns . . . .

"Four. Four I have. Do I hear five?"

The voice rises and falls, tuneless, magnetic. Toes twitch to the rhythm. Knitting needles take it up. Children slow down on their soft drinks to listen. The men move closer.

"Five. Five I have. Do I hear six?"

Invariably somebody loses his head.

"Two I have from this gentleman in the back. Who'll make it three?"

"Three," the same gentleman will shout, red-faced, in answer, determined not to give way to anyone.

I remember one time when two sisters, sitting apart, bid furiously on the same cut-glass bowl. "Why did you keep forcing me up?" one asked hotly, coming over to the other when the bidding finally stopped.

"I wanted you to be sure and get it," the sister said.

And I remember a young couple, homeless, heading across the country on a motorcycle, who had just stopped for a minute to look on but couldn't resist bidding, and found themselves the bewildered possessors of a mammoth, golden-oak dining-room set piled high by the roadside, awaiting removal.

The crowd relishes it all, peering at every purchase, offering advice or approval, sometimes doing a little trading on their own, thus relieving themselves of articles for which their enthusiasm has already cooled. Maybe a paperweight showing Mount Vernon for two finger bowls. Or a hobnailed pitcher and three matching glasses for a kerosene camp stove. Or a pair of bottle-green portieres and a spray of plastic roses for a folding cot.

Meanwhile the men are carrying things to the cars. Washtubs. Dry sinks. Whatnots. Wagon seats. Cobblers' benches. Bureaus, empty of drawers. Cabinets, with doors swinging. A horsehair sofa, hard to grasp. Schoolroom desks. A lawn swing or two. Church pews. Maybe an organ. And always near the end of the procession some patient husband tussles resignedly with a spinnng wheel.

Oh, there's nothing quite so heady on a summer day as a seat in some farmyard, facing a faded, dusty, odorous helter-skelter of almost everything in which who knows what may be hiding, and hearing at the same time the hypnotic, coercing voice of the auctioneer.

"Four. Four I have. Do I hear five?"

A House in Maine

he house stands on the side of a hill (Heart Broke Hill, the first deed calls it) at the head of a narrow cove, like an aisle, where the tide marches in from the Sheepscot. It is a very old house, and it stands alone, secluded, crowded on three sides by the forest.

Taken by itself there is nothing unusual about it — a Cape Cod house, white with green blinds framing its low windows. New England abounds in such houses. But this one, shaped to the land, seems almost to have been created with its surroundings.

It faces south, shaded by two enormous maples. From its dooryard, overgrown with lilies, you can watch the water come in, spreading until it washes the roots of the evergreens that line the shore. At high tide fish hawks sail with the air currents, soar, flutter, then hit the surface with a heavy splash. At low tide, gulls circle or walk, switching over the flats. Herons stand motionless, or lift their long legs daintily, or soar off on their great wings. Occasionally a porcupine lumbers from one side of the cove to the other, and sometimes in the early morning a deer comes to drink from the brook that makes a path over the shining, pewter-colored flats.

To the north the hill rises higher, matted with uncut hay and shaggy with juniper. In summer a few wild flowers color it — buttercups, wood lilies, ox-eyed daisies, vetch. In fall it is burnished with scrub oaks and brightened with maples. On its very top, precipitous with ledges, are six giant spruces. Standing beneath them and looking down, you see a thread of road, grey among greenness, four roofs, widely separated and, directly below, the house itself, trim, symmetrical—a house, it seems, in miniature.

Close to it, the past seems all about. You feel it in the rutted driveway, once the country road; in the old garden behind the shed, taken over by clover but still brightened by a stock or two of Sweet William, not yet run out; in the orchard where, except in May or June when they blossom, a dozen ancient apple trees are all but obscured by pine and sumac; in the hand-hewn timbers of the old barn, lying hit or miss like a pile of jackstraws. You see it in the old door rocks, worn smooth by many crossings. You feel it around the shore where once a village stood.

Sitting on one of the great stones and looking north, you see, half a mile as the gulls fly, the house on Heart Broke Hill — small, resolute, standing its ground against the forest. Its size, its whiteness, its perfect harmony to setting make you feel, especially in the evening when the sun sinks early behind the hill, almost a sense of enchantment.

The past is inside, too. You smell it when you open

the door — sweet and spicy and sour, full of dry rot and creosote and dampness. It is as though everything that had ever been in the house had left its scent there. Beets and turnips and apples stored in the cellar. Fresh-churned butter. Vinegar and kerosene and molasses. Old clothing. Wood ashes. The brine used to pickle pork. Let in the sun and wind and it fades a little, but close the door for half an hour and it is all back.

You can see the age of the house quite readily. It is in the broad fireplaces, the hand-hewn corner posts, the carved woodwork, the hand-forged latches, in the knots that protrude from the wide boards of the floor. But to see the past itself you must look closer. At the worn thresholds and the depressions in the narrow stairs. At the hollows in the floor by the sink and stove. At the top of the old kitchen table, scarred by knives and burned by pots and kettles. At the lid of the old woodbox, its edge worn thin by many liftings.

You not only smell the past and see it, you feel it almost as a presence. Entering, you hear your voice change to that of a visitor. It is impossible, even when you are away from the house, to think of it as empty.

Behind the house stands the shed, whose narrow front door lets in a dim light. By it you can see a floorless area piled with wood, on top of which lies a tangle of fish line and a clam hod holding a rusty hoe. Among the chips and sawdust that surround it, frail, limp blackberry vines struggle to grow. Hanging from the walls are old harnesses, old chains, old saws, old hoops, old shovels and rakes. Beyond is the watercloset, protruding from the shed itself like a child's bottom.

A heavy, handmade ladder leads to the loft. It is dim here, too, for the window is heavily curtained with dust. Every generation has left something. A great rusted saw from an old mill. A carpenter's bench with an enormous wooden vise. Wagon hubs. The rusted frame of a lantern. In the center of it all is a sleigh, still looking rather dashing with a whip in its socket and bells on its shafts. Leaning against it is an old four-posted bed, its ropes frayed and sagging. Old doors stand slantingly against the walls. Old trunks squat in every corner, their straps rotting. Cobwebs drip everywhere. Stand still and you will hear mice runnning . . .

The barn is only a sunken ruin encircled by its underpinning of granite blocks. It looks treacherous, and it is — a heap of rotting beams and board and rafters lying every which way, laced with rusty hoops and pierced with iron bars. You need stout shoes to explore it. You need quick eyes and a sense of balance, too.

A portion of the old floor is there, its cracks still filled with hayseed. There, tilted, is the splintered section of a decaying door, its button intact on its square iron nail. Beyond is a battered horse sled, a frame for the wild blackberries to lean on. A paintless whippletree protrudes from a bed of fresh green ferns. Strawberry plants grow through knotholes of decaying timbers. Where the manure pile stood, touch-me-nots grow lush and abundant.

Animal life is everywhere. If you lift up a board, a multitude of carpenter ants will swarm in every direction. Earwigs will scurry off, earthworms stir sluggishly. Step on a rotting plank and a field mouse may bound away or a snake glide out of sight. At dusk you are likely to surprise a skunk digging for insects or a porcupine eating the greenery. Something is always moving there . . .

There is almost always a wind on Heart Broke Hill. On fair days it comes from the south, stirring the day lilies that grow beneath the low windows, hustling the but-

terflies. Stronger, it ruffles the feathers of the birds on the telephone wires and loosens the straw from their nests in the maples.

Generally it is a warm wind, smelling in spring of lilacs and apple blossoms, in summer of phlox and hay mixed with the resinous smell of pine and the tang of the shore. Sometimes, shifting to the east, it brings the faint, fading smell of Bouncing Bets around the well.

When the tide is rising, the water comes in dreamily, bearing petals of foam. When it turns, men will come with hoes and hods for clamming, or pails and burlap bags for worms and for the weeds in which to ship them. While they work, sandpipers scurry, unperturbed, about them, and, if it is late afternoon, gulls fly casually above the light from the setting sun reflected on their bellies. The weeders are the last to go, their bulging bags slung over their shoulders, looking like gnomes and leaving long, irregular trails behind them. By sundown the shore is deserted.

Not every day is fair on Heart Broke Hill. Sometimes there is a fog. You can watch it coming, first dimming the mouth of the cove, then the neighbor's dock, then your own shore. If the weather has been hot or dry, you welcome it for the restfulness it brings. It brings quiet, too. There is no wind at all. Lines relax. Colors soften. Tensions dissolve. Cobwebs appear in the grass, hang from the clothesline. The grapes on the grapevine shine.

Most fogs disappear by noon, but now and then one settles in and stays stubbornly. Moisture gathers on the windows and flows down in little rivulets. The cookstove smokes, and the newly starched curtains grow limp. Dish towels hang all day on the rod of the stove and still will not dry. The organ keys stick, as do the bureau drawers. In the front hall the wallpaper buckles. Looking toward the road, you see nothing but the trunks of the maples, and you hear nothing but the drip of fog from their branches. Step out the front door and the bittersweet vine, shaken, drenches you. You see only what is at your feet. Above and beyond is fog.

And there are days of extreme heat. Before the sun is up, locusts start singing. There are no clouds in the sky and the cove is still. Two days of this and the lupins droop. The vine hangs limp over the kitchen window. The rowboat turns aimlessly, nosing the shore.

A week, and the grass turns brown. Dust coats the alders and obscures the license plates of the few cars that pass. Worried about the well, you stop watering the garden.

The lupins wither. The phlox grow brittle. Only the grapevine thrives. When you pump at the sink, you hear the water soak into the dry earth around it. It is hot in the house, too — unbearable in the chambers.

Early one evening static begins on the radio. Birds suddenly appear and fly excitedly about. The sky darkens and thunderheads gather behind the hill. Lightning flashes throughout the house. Sitting tensely by the parlor window, you remind yourself how old the house is, how long it has stood. Thunder mounts, breaks, reverberates. Lightning sharpens, slashing the sky. Darkness deepens. The wind rises, rattling the windows. Trees stir and bend. With each flash you can see every line and ledge of the cove. With each surge of wind, dead branches snap and fall.

You wait, eyes closed, ears blocked. A flash that nothing can shut out and with it a crash that sets the whole house shaking. Then the rain, the belated rain, starts falling.

The houses that remain around the cove are summer houses now. It is the middle of June before the shutters come from their windows and caps from their chimneys. Then station wagons begin to run back and forth along the road to the village. Boats with outboards appear on the shore, and lawn chairs brighten the shrinking dooryards. City dogs bark half the night at country noises.

The season is too short. There seems no time for major projects. No time to restore the outbuildings, to rebuild the stone walls, to repair the driveway, or to haul away the ruins of the old barn. No time to prune the apple trees. No time to clean out the shed. There is time only to sweep up the dead flies and spiders. To drive out the mice and clean the rust from the cookstove. To rake up the dead leaves, to mow the grass, to spray the nests of tent caterpillars.

Time only to pick blueberries on the hillside, the sun on your back, or, pail held high, to hunt for raspberries among the underbrush in the pasture. Time for swimming at the junction of the coves where, when the tide ebbs, the waters have a force to be reckoned with. Time to row to one of the ledges, tide-covered except for a few hours of the day, and sit, knees drawn up, watching the sea birds until the water rises to your feet.

Then the summer is over. The rowboat is pulled up. The shutters go back on. The chimney is recapped. By the middle of September everything is quiet again. Only the hunters travel the road. Only the wormers swinging their pails, the clammers their hods, and the weeders, their bags over their shoulders, follow the silent shore.

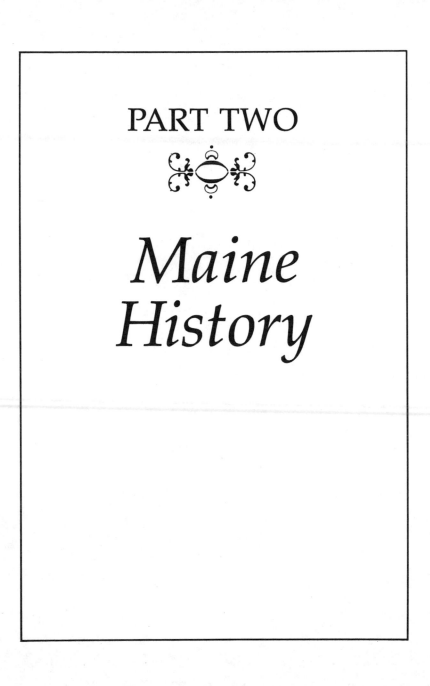

PART TWO

Maine History

Maine History

he stories that follow — one set on the land, one set on the sea — are among the most dramatic in Maine history. Both are carefully researched from original or official records. That of the *Portland* disaster is — as far as the author can determine — the only complete and authenticated account that has been written.

M.S.

A Loyalist
of the
Kennebec

ne story of the American Revolution is seldom told. It is the story of those men and women (one out of three, John Adams estimated) who remained loyal to the British Crown. Some took their stand because of old roots and traditions; some because they feared a business loss; some because they believed that by legal means and patience the breach could be satisfactorily healed. Whatever their reasons and whatever their stations, all suffered the same persecution. Their houses were plundered; their barns were burned; their livestock was slaughtered.

Though they had little of material worth to lose, few suffered more than the clergymen of the Church of England, who, almost unanimously, despite threats and abuse and calumny, remained steadfast in their loyalty to their conscience and their King. One of them was Jacob Bailey.

Jacob Bailey was born in Rowley, Massachusetts, in 1731. A shy, sensitive boy, he grew up in an environment where "politeness was ridiculed, learning scorned." Though extremely religious by nature, he was early troubled by the fact that members of the local church, where his father was a deacon, demanded freedom of worship for themselves, yet denied it to others.

Feeling apart from his contemporaries, he spent his free time writing both verse and prose. One of his pages, mislaid, reached the eyes of the local minister, a kindly, charitable man, who, impressed by its quality, offered to teach the boy without charge. When he was almost twenty, the two of them traveled from possible patron to patron, covering nearly all of New England, until they had accumulated enough money and goods ("A pair of gloves . . . A yard and a half of fine muslin and a pair of worsted stockings . . . ") for him to enter Harvard.

He entered a distinguished class. John Adams, later to become President, was in it, and Jonathan Wentworth, who would be Governor of New Hampshire. Both were his friends. There were also two future judges of the Massachusetts Supreme Court, a future senator, and a future president of Harvard College. And, ominously, there were two other men, Charles Cushing and Jonathan Bowman, who, years later, were to dedicate themselves to Bailey's ruin.

After his graduation in 1755, at the foot of his class — placing then being determined solely by social position — he began teaching school in Kingston, New Hampshire. Still timid and gauche, he was, nevertheless, searching for fresh and broader experiences. He did not find them. The people were dull, he complained. The conversation was "sooty." All around him "Drinking, Sabbath-breaking, and immodesty prevailed."

Disheartened, he gave up one school after another until finally in Hampton, New Hampshire, he found an environment sufficiently congenial to hold him. Here he stayed two years, unbending enough to appreciate the "easy, ingenuous young ladies." One of them was Sarah Weeks, his scholar, whom he was later to marry.

Even in this environment his mind was constantly troubled by the impiety he saw about him — the profanity, the sexual promiscuity, the irreverence, and inattention at public worship. Thus it is not strange that he should have decided to go into the ministry. Since the only church he knew was the Congregational, he "overcame his bashful humor" sufficiently to apply for a license to preach. Barely had he received it when he learned of a vacancy for a minister in the Church of England.

He applied for it at once, despite the objections of his parents. Why he did this, his journals do not reveal. No doubt he was reacting from the bigotry he had known as a child. No doubt, too, he had found in the form and ritual of this church some grace and dignity he had not found before. And having chafed all his life against provincialism, he welcomed an opportunity for travel.

For to be ordained he must cross the sea to England. This he did in a ship named *The Hind*, where for twenty-eight days he shared a greasy canvas hammock with a man-servant of one of the passengers, constantly disturbed by the fumes of pitch, the foul smell of bilge water, and the persecutions of the sailors who criticized his manner of speaking and sought to tempt him into "some fashionable excess."

Once faced with the grandeur of London and especially Westminster Abbey, he forgot the discomforts of the crossing. His examination (in English, Latin, and Greek) easily passed, he was feasted by the Bishop of Rochester on plates which in his innocent mind appeared to be of solid gold. He dined twice with Benjamin Franklin — "a gentleman of good education," he recorded, "who has passed away the flower of his youth in too many extravagances." Finally he was ordained as a Frontier Missionary on a salary of fifty pounds, a sum beyond his "most sanguine expectations," and assigned to the region of the Kennebec.

When he arrived there in July, 1760, he found approximately seven thousand inhabitants, English, Irish, French, and German. All were poor. All suffered from the sparseness of the soil, the rigor of the seasons, and the perils of the wilderness, still stirring with hostile Indians. Many were illiterate. Many lived in miserable huts without chimneys, sleeping on heaps of straw and subsisting for months at a time on clams and potatoes. Few had Bibles. Yet they were not indifferent to religion, for they had petitioned most fervently for a missionary to be sent to their "truly necessitous place," promising to build him a church and parsonage. And they received him with warmth.

He settled in Frankfort (later to become Pownalborough, still later to be divided into Dresden, Alna, and Wiscasset), making his headquarters at Fort Shirley on the river. At once he began his mission. Sometimes he traveled as many as fifty miles at a stretch, on foot and by canoe in all weather, suffering in winter from hunger and exposure, assaulted in summer by great swarms of flies and mosquitoes. He preached, he married, he baptized, he buried. At the end of a year a superior in the church who visited him and watched his work gave praise for "his diligence, prudence and exemplary conduct." Encouraged, and relying on the promise of a church and parsonage, he returned to New Hampshire and married Sarah Weeks, not yet fifteen.

About this time Pownalborough was incorporated and became the county seat. A new courthouse, three stories high, went up, facing the river. New settlers came — men with money to invest, merchants, lawyers. New houses were built, new wharves, new stores. There was an aristocracy now, made up of men who wanted power and had come to the frontier to get it, especially at the expense of the poorer settlers, many of whom still did not speak English.

Quick to seize this power were two men from Massachusetts — Charles Cushing and Jonathan Bowman. Quick to oppose their attempts was Jacob Bailey, who had been graduated at the foot of their class at Harvard.

Having no grounds on which they could oppose him openly, they struck at him through his church. Themselves members of the Congregational Church — the official church in Massachusetts — they attended his services only to cause disturbance, using boyish tricks to make the women smile, reading audibly from a primer instead of a prayer book, putting soap, scraps of paper, once even a pack of cards into the collection plate. They scratched out sentences from the new Common Prayer sent by the Society and wrote heretical material in the margins.

Through all this Bailey kept his head, going about his baptisms and his burials. His congregation was growing, numbering regularly from fifty to one hundred fifty. He had, moreover, congregations at Harpswell, Georgetown, and Richmond. In the rare moments he was at home (a log house now) he taught himself French that he might talk with the French settlers in their own tongue. He began to write a history of the region and to make a study of its minerals. He tended his garden where he grew fruits "delicious rich and rare"; berries of all kinds; daffodils, crocuses, tulips, wild flowers — even arbutus, transplanted from the wilderness. He wrote verses. Crowded now with his growing family, he sighed for the church and parsonage which had been promised him.

Ten years he waited for them. Every time a move was made to start them, Cushing and Bowman managed to divert it. When they could delay things no longer, they worked out another scheme. Once the buildings were up (the parsonage was never completely finished), Bowman claimed the land on which they stood. He threatened those who came to services and announced his intention of putting a chimney in the church and renting it for a dwelling. Bailey took the case to court, which Bowman controlled, and lost it. He was forced to pay a lease until eventually a higher court upheld him.

When difficulties arose between the King and the colonies, Bailey chose to remain loyal to the King. Like all ministers of the Church of England, he had taken a vow to uphold the Crown, and it was inconceivable to him that he should break it. Besides, he felt contempt for the self-called Sons of Liberty, who had already begun a campaign of persecution against the Loyalists, assaulting persons and property. When a man in nearby Falmouth said that

128

in his opinion the Stamp Act was right and reasonable, his store had been pulled down and he himself had been tarred and feathered. Bailey spoke out in his defense. He spoke out again when all the tea in the area was seized and dumped into the river at Georgetown.

Here was the ammunition that Cushing and Bowman had been waiting for, and they lost no time in using it. In the summer of 1774 they invaded the parsonage with "100 men in arms, delivering threats." Doors and windows were broken. Manuscripts were torn into bits. The new garden, far more extensive than the old — indeed, the finest, it was generally agreed, this side of Boston — was trampled and uprooted.

Confused, yet still adamant in his stand against what he considered to be anarchy, Bailey started out for Boston to find out what was happening there. What he found out must have shocked him. Refugees from all directions were pouring into the city, seeking British protection. They bore harrowing tales of pillage and abuse. Buildings had been burned, women stripped, livestock tortured. Returning, Bailey himself was mobbed at Brunswick and obliged to flee for his life.

Home again, half of the time in hiding, he managed to go on with his work. He had no salary now. Seven of his twelve sheep had been killed by the Sons of Liberty and his fine heifer shot as it grazed in his pasture. Cushing, recently elected sheriff, and Bowman, now clerk of courts, had threatened anyone who should give his family supplies. Under their threats, his congregation diminished.

The day word came of the Battle of Lexington, Bailey was seized near his home and assaulted by a crowd of ruffians. Two days later the same crowd, augmented, noisily prevented his wife's brother, a clergyman of the Church of England at Marblehead, from landing with his

129

wife and eight children, seeking refuge with Bailey until he could move to property he himself owned along the river. Eventually he was allowed to come ashore, but not until he had been compelled to sign "an ignominious paper." That night a ruffian attempted to fire his gun into the parsonage. It failed to go off, though later on the green it discharged easily.

Jacob Bailey was not the only Loyalist in the area, nor was he the only one to be persecuted. Many, notably the weakest, had already been brought to trial and con- demned to exile. Many more had fled to places of their own choosing, leaving their property behind to be seized at once by the Sons of Liberty, who did a thorough job of it. One of those who fled was Captain Charles Callahan, a member of Bailey's congregation. Bowman, as clerk of courts, demanded that the captain's wife render an account of all his effects. She refused and was thrown in jail. When later she escaped and fled, the Sons of Liberty seized "the very flax she had raised and dressed with her own hands, the fowls about the door — even a canary bird and cage."

In September, 1775, Benedict Arnold sailed up the Kennebec on his way to Quebec. Two hundred bateaux, hurriedly built, were awaiting his arrival. Fervor among the Sons of Liberty grew. Bailey wisely went into hiding. In October the British burned Falmouth, now Portland. It was a savage, senseless act. Sober, responsible citizens, already tried by the blockade of Boston and angered by their expulsion from their fishing grounds, now joined the Sons of Liberty because it was the only organization ready for action. And the time for action, they decided, had come.

On New Year's Day a liberty pole was erected on the village green. Someone suggested that Bailey be con- ducted by military force from the parsonage and be compel- led to consecrate it. A vote was taken, and by a small majority he was spared. However, that night the pole was knocked from its base. Bailey was accused of having done it. He instantly issued a stinging denial. But the incident had its effect, and his congregation, already shrinking, grew smaller.

For some months Cushing and Bowman had been bringing Congregationalists into the community. In March, 1776, though they had no minister and no meeting house, they pronounced their church to be the only lawful one, asserting that only its members had a right to vote on public issues and that all inhabitants would be taxed for its support. Those who would not pay, they warned, would have their cattle seized and sold at auction.

Most people paid as a way of keeping out of further trouble. Their troubles were already heavy. Bailey himself describes the state of affairs in that area in a letter sent to a friend in Massachusetts in March 1776:

> Those who retain any sentiments of tenderness and humanity, when acquainted with the circumstances of this eastern country, must compassionate our situation: a people confined to a cold and rugged soil, encumbered with forests and divided by rivers, exposed to invasions from Canada, deprived of free navigation, prevented from selling, as usual, their timber for the necessities of life, and denied the advantages of receiving provisions from abroad as formerly. These occurrences have reduced us all . . .to the lowest conditions of poverty and almost to nakedness and famine.

Though others weakened under pressure, Bailey without salary, his livestock killed, his garden ruined, did not. In spite of threats, he preached regularly and he refused to omit mention of the King in his prayers. Other ministers of his church, including his brother-in-law, had

131

compromised here, but Bailey was a resolute man. He had taken his stand, and he would keep it. Several months later he refused to read the Declaration of Independence from his pulpit. A warrant was issued for his arrest, and once more he went into hiding.

Warned of a plot against his life, he left home again in October, and, under the cover of fog, escaped by canoe to Brunswick, where he begged a horse and started for Boston. There, learning of the alliance with the French, he was obliged to face the fact that he was on the losing side. Yet to him it was the right side, and, whatever came of it, he resolved never to waver. Friends gave him money, and he arrived home in time for Christmas, still convinced of "the obstinacy, the folly, the madness, and the perfidy" of his countrymen.

For six months he faced the bullying of the Congregationalists and the mounting molestations of the Sons of Liberty. Then, his money spent, his family subsisting only on "ground-roots" he decided they must leave the area and seek refuge with other Loyalists in Nova Scotia, where his brother-in-law had already fled. In July he started for Boston to make the necessary arrangements. Not without some humor he described his attire:

> . . . an old rusty threadbare black coat which had been turned and the buttonholes worked with thread almost white, with a number of breaches about the elbows; a jacket of the same, much fractured about the buttonholes and hanging loose, occasioned by the leanness of my carcasss . . . greatly emaciated by the constant exercise of temperance; a pair of breeches constructed of coarse bed-tick, of a dirty yellow color . . . a perpendicular patch upon each knee of a different complexion from the original piece . . . a hat with many holes in the brim, adorned with much darning.

He petitioned the General Court for the permission

he needed. Then, again furnished with money by friends, he returned home to find his family in great distress, for during his absence it had been made a criminal offense for anyone to assist them. Waiting for him was a notice from Cushing, the sheriff, informing him that he could no longer officiate in his church and threatening him with imprisonment should he do so.

Shut out of his church, he nevertheless continued to preach in the area whenever his services were requested. On one occasion, returning home from a service, he was assaulted by a violent mob, armed with axes and clubs, and stripped naked.

Finding out that he wanted to leave, Cushing and Bowman did all they could to prevent his departure, determined either to imprison him or force him to take an oath of allegiance to Congress. Because of their influence, his first petition, pleading conscience, was denied. His second, pleading poverty, was granted, but not until the winter of 1778.

He could not leave at once. The weather was bad. No ship was immediately available. So in spite of Cushing's warning, he continued to minister to his remaining parishioners, who had made a formal request that he do so. Once when he was visiting a sickroom, Cushing appeared in the kitchen and was only prevented from dragging him out by the interference of a servant. Again, reinforced with a gang, Cushing noisily interrupted a funeral which he was conducting. But for the alertness of friends who hid him, he would surely have been taken and imprisoned.

On June 7 he and his family started toward the shore with their few possessions: "two ancient feather beds, through the weather-beaten crevices of which the down issued in great abundance; one patched quilt, containing a greater variety of colors than the rainbow; half of a very elderly rug, worn to the quick, and half a pair of sheets, and a small chest, containing the remnants of poverty."

On the way friends joined them for a sad farewell, bearing gifts — a slice of salmon, a jar of butter — taken from their slender stores. One brought a child for baptism. At the wharf a small boat, manned by Bailey's parishioners, was ready to take them to Georgetown, where a schooner waited.

After prayers came the parting. The boat pushed off, and standing at the stern, his eyes on the shores of the Kennebec where he had labored so long, where one of his children now lay, Bailey felt an anguish in his heart.

As the months passed, the anguish softened. In Nova Scotia he became chaplain of a British regiment. For the first time in almost twenty years he knew security. His home was comfortable, his garden unmolested. He had no fear of spies, no need to think of hiding. His children prospered.

He lived until 1808, and died, so the story goes, still praying for his King.

Shipwreck

he sky was overcast when the steamer *Portland* left India Wharf in Boston at seven o'clock on Saturday evening, November 26,1898, and headed for the open sea. Built in 1890, she was a wooden sidewheeler, one of the best of her kind on the New England coast. Everything about her showed workmanship and quality. Her hull was constructed of white oak, yellow pine, and hackmatack. Her frame was strapped with iron belting. She had, moreover, an air of elegance. On her upper deck was a fine saloon, carpeted in red and handsomely furnished with matching sofas. Leading to the dining room below was a graceful curved staircase. She was lighted with cut-glass chandeliers.

A good-sized steamer, her length was 280.9 feet; her tonnage, 2,283; her horsepower, 1,500; her speed, twelve knots. She ran alternately with her sister ship, the *Bay State*, the nine-hour trip between Portland and Boston, carrying up to 500 passengers and a crew of from forty to fifty.

On that November day the weather forecast, released at noon, was threatening but not ominous.

> For Boston and vicinity: Snow tonight and Sunday morning, followed by clearing and much colder weather. Winds becoming easterly and increasing in force, and shifting to northwest.
>
> For Maine, New Hampshire and Vermont: Heavy snow and warmer tonight. Sunday, snow and much colder. Southeasterly winds, shifting by tonight to northeasterly gales.

At the mouth of the harbor she met the steamer *Kennebec*, which, having started and turned back, tooted a warning. It was not the *Portland*'s first warning. Earlier a telephone call had come from Captain Dennison of the *Bay State*, saying that he would stay in port and advising Captain Blanchard to do the same. Another call had come from Mr. Liscomb, manager of the line, instructing Captain Blanchard not to sail at seven, but to wait until nine before making his decision. Unable to reach Captain Blanchard, Mr. Liscomb had given his message to Mr. Williams, agent of the line, asking him to pass it on. But at seven the whistle had blown. The late arrivals, congratulating themselves on their good luck, had rushed up the gangplank. One of them, Captain Albert Dunbar of Boothbay Harbor, had quite literally jumped aboard.

By the time the *Portland* reached the harbor's mouth, snow had begun falling. She acknowledged the signal from the *Kennebec*, but kept right on toward the open sea.

Within, the passengers must have begun to settle themselves for the voyage. Some, tired out, probably went at once to their cabins; others doubtless went to the dining room to enjoy a late supper, with perhaps some of the champagne the steamer carried. A few hardy ones may have walked the deck, turning their collars against the

136

snow, which was already brisk and business-like. But most of them must have gathered in the red-carpeted saloon to read the evening papers picked up in Boston, or to lounge in the red plush armchairs while looking over the other passengers.

It was a quiet, well bred group, made up for the most part of Maine people who had been spending Thanksgiving with relatives in Boston. There were professional and business men: two were lawyers; one was a jeweler; several were owners or managers of factories. There were women on family errands: two had been staying with sick relatives; three were on their way to attend funerals. There were six teachers returning to their classes. There were laborers, too — a sailor, a driver, a dozen or so factory workers anticipating a Sunday with their families in Portland.

A good many young people were aboard. There were two college boys, one of them George Kenniston, of Boothbay Harbor; there were four or five young clerks, and about the same number of salesmen. There were several young ladies, two of them students of music. One was a high school girl who had pressed her mother into returning on Saturday so that she might not be late for school on Monday morning. One was a girl of twenty-two whose fiancé had been killed two months before in the Spanish-American War.

Fathers, young themselves, had their children with them. Oren Hooper of Portland had taken his son Carl up to Worcester to visit the Mechanics Fair. William Chase, who had organized the fair, was himself on board, with his son Philip. Isaiah Fry had his eight-year-old daughter, Ruth, with him. Some had their entire families. Frank Pierce, whose wife and two children had been visiting in Massachusetts, was bringing them back home. George Heald was traveling with his wife and child; so also was

Charles Thompson of Woodsford. Jessen Schmidt, a Dane, had taken his wife and two children, aged four and five, back for a visit to his native country. Now they were on the last lap of their long journey.

Among the passengers were three distinguished men. One was the Honorable E. Dudley Freeman, Amherst, 1875, a lawyer and an author from Yarmouth, who had been a state senator, chairman of the Republican District Committee and a member of the Governor's Council. Another was James Flower, who only two weeks before had come from St. Johns to Lewiston, to become principal of Bliss Business College. Only thirty-nine years old, he was a graduate of Harvard College and of Boston University Law School. Another was Henry DeMerritt Young, a distinguished and well-loved Boston artist, only thirty-four, on his way with his finest paintings to give an exhibition of them in Portland. Ironically, most of them were of the sea.

As is the way of travelers, they must have picked up and passed on the gossip of the ship. Those from Portland, where he lived, knew Captain Blanchard, at least by reputation, and that was good. They knew that he had been on the line nine years and only recently promoted from pilot to captain. Some of them, no doubt, knew his wife and three children. Perhaps a few knew that his brother had died at sea two months before en route to Hong Kong. Some may have overheard that the crew was short-handed, that three men — the First Pilot, the First Mate, and the Purser's clerk — had stayed on shore to attend the funeral of an official of the line; that the boy in the Purser's office was a checker on the company's wharf, assigned as a substitute.

While they talked, or ate, or rested in their cabins, the wind was rising. By nine o'clock the sea was really rough. Bells must have been ringing as, feeling the motion, passengers requested a lemon or a piece of pilot bread. Stewardesses must have hurried about with trays, while stewards lashed the furniture and strung up life lines. Passengers still in the saloon probably debated whether to stay up longer or to try sleeping. Those who decided to go below must have found they could walk only with difficulty. Had they wanted to try a turn on deck, and been allowed to, they would have found they could not walk at all.

But the steamer kept to her course. A number of schooners saw her. At nine-thirty the *Maude S.*, hurrying for Gloucester Harbor, passed her. At eleven when the wind was stronger and the snow so thick as almost to preclude visibility, the *Grayling* barely avoided a collision with her. At that time she was observed to be in normal condition, though, like every other boat caught on the open sea, rolling and pitching badly.

Probably even then the passengers felt no real apprehension. It was winter. New Englanders were used to blizzards, and they had all, at one time or another, experienced rough seas. But there must have been anxiety on the bridge, for the wind was a gale then, and a look at the barometer would have shown it already low and rapidly falling. Captain Blanchard must have long before this realized the folly of his decision. But once out in the open sea he could not have turned back a side-wheel steamer like the *Portland* without damage. So he apparently had determined to do the only sensible thing — to make for a harbor. This harbor was probably Gloucester, for at 11:45 the captain of the *Edgar Randall* saw what he believed to be the *Portland* headed westward. In fact, he barely avoided a collision with her. Her superstructure was damaged, he noticed, and she had no lights. Before he could see any more the snow had shut her off completely. Meanwhile the storm was sweeping the entire northeastern coast.

139

Winds blowing up to a hundred miles an hour toppled chimneys, ripped off shutters, snapped telephone poles, shook steeples. Great trees, uprooted, fell.

Snow smothered everything. It blocked all traffic. Trolleys stopped on their tracks. Cabs and bakers' carts and milk wagons, deserted, littered the streets. Trains — even elevated trains — stopped running. Freight cars piled up in wrecks. Wires fell. Boston was entirely isolated from the suburbs, some of which lay under drifts of fifteen and twenty feet.

The tide was higher than it had ever been in anyone's memory. It carried off cottages. It covered the piers in some places up to four feet, washing away beams and planks. It loosened the foundations of storehouses. It flooded cellars and damaged merchandise. In Boston it wrecked the subway.

That night from New York to eastern Maine one hundred vessels were lost, many of them having been dashed against the shores of the harbors where they had sought refuge. Thirty-five of them lay wrecked on the islands of Boston Harbor.

What a night of terror that must have been on board the *Portland*, with the force of the wind that tore off timbers; the violence of the waves, breaking through the portholes; the shifting of heavy cargo.

There must have been pale faces, hoarse whispers. Hands must have trembled as they tied on life belts, then gripped on to anything that would hold. There must have been sickness, broken bones, bad bruises.

When the lights went out, there must have been some panic and a great many prayers. Everyone must have known the danger then, known that lifeboats, even had they not been swept away, could never be launched on such a sea. Their only hope, they must have known, lay

140

in the ship's staying afloat. And on everyone's lips must have been the same question: Will the ship hold together? By some miracle will she get through?

The night passed and the ship still floated, though far off her course and perilously near the treacherous Peaked Hill Bar. Her engines must have been going, for otherwise she would have swung broadside and faced the end. But her situation was desperate.

Around five o'clock in the morning Captain Fisher of the Race Point Life Saving Station, on the tip of Cape Cod, heard four faint blasts of a steamer's whistle — the signal of distress. He struck his bell, sent up rockets, and ran out his lifeboat. Then he waited for another sound to guide him, but none came.

A little later the storm halted momentarily and the captain of the schooner *Ruth M. Martin*, fighting to keep his own ship afloat, caught a glimpse of the *Portland*, heading toward the open sea. Then the storm closed in once more.

No one ever saw her again.

The storm lasted thirty hours. On Monday morning people began to dig themselves out. It took 5,000 horses to clear the streets of New York, 4,000 men to shovel before an elevated train could start running in Boston. There was, of course, no train or mail service. (The first train from New York reached Boston on Monday afternoon, the first from Portland on Tuesday morning after a trip requiring twenty-five hours.) But late Monday morning the *Boston Journal* appeared on the streets reporting the storm, the worst, it claimed, since the blizzard of 1851. On the front page, among the statistics of winds and drifts and temperatures, was a brief bulletin regarding the *Portland*, revealing that she was long overdue.

On the same page was this reassuring note from the steamship company:

> Note: People having friends on board the steamer *Portland* when she sailed from Boston Saturday evening should not become alarmed for the safety of the vessel as yet. Telephonic and telegraphic communications with ports along the north shore, particularly Gloucester, where the captain of the *Portland* would be most likely to head her for shelter from the storm, is entirely cut off, and for that reason no word can be obtained as to the *Portland*'s whereabouts.
>
> It is not unlikely that the big steamer headed back for Boston when she ran into the storm Saturday night and is now anchored in a sheltered spot down the harbor, for no tugs dared venture very far down on Saturday, and, owing to falling snow, a good view of what was down below could not be obtained.

A few hours later the *Bay State* came in on her regular trip, having kept a sharp watch on the way. She had seen no trace of the *Portland*, nor had the *State of Maine*, arriving later in the day. By afternoon the offices of the company on both ends of the line were crowded with anxious rela-

142

tives, waiting for news. At four o'clock communications were established with Gloucester. The *Portland* had not been seen or heard of there. At once arrangements were made for the revenue cutters *Woodbury*, from Portland, and *Dallas*, from Boston, to search for the missing steamer.

On the wharves the crowds grew. On India Wharf relatives besieged the officials for a passenger list, each hoping against hope that his sister or brother or cousin had missed the boat, being somehow deterred. But the company had no list; it was on board the *Portland*. By this time the number of relatives belied the company's estimate of twenty-five to thirty passengers. There were so many relatives they overflowed the offices and used the saloon on the *Bay State* until she sailed. All night on both ends of the line the offices kept open. People sat and walked and sat again. On India Wharf Clerk Dudley did all he could, and his kindness is still remembered. But nothing could relieve the awful uncertainty.

Could it — could it be?

There was no uncertainty on Cape Cod. On Sunday afternoon people there knew as much as ever could be known about the steamer's fate. Around one o'clock the first wreckage had appeared — a few battered trunks and barrels. Then a plank came in bearing the number 2293, the tonnage mark of the *Portland*. At four o'clock the body of a man, a Negro, wearing a steward's badge, was washed ashore at North Truro. Within an hour three other bodies followed at nearby points. Then more wreckage — a creamery can; fragments of timber; barrels of lard; cigars; piano keys; the ship's wheel (probably an emergency wheel) lashed with twelve fathoms of wire; water-soaked cheeses; a life raft; a gold-headed cane; life preservers marked *Stmr. Portland*, probably ineptly tied and torn off by the sea. Not a spar washed up was as long as a man's arm.

143

Before dark, other bodies came in. All along the shore people waded into the treacherous surf to get them. Some of the bodies wore life belts over heavy clothing, as if prepared for disaster; some, washed out of their cabins, were in night attire; some had their clothing completely torn away. All were frozen and mutilated. A few wore watches which had stopped between nine and ten o'clock, establishing the time of the disaster.

How to get the news to Boston? Wires were down. No trains were running, for tracks were undermined for more than a mile between Provincetown and Truro and again between Chatham and Sandwich. Safe travel by sea was still out of the question. The telegraph operator at Truro tried constantly to get through, but it was Monday afternoon before he was able, momentarily, to send out a faint message.

Charles Ward, a Chatham correspondent for the *Boston Herald* who happened to be in Hyannis, heard just enough to know that the *Portland* had been wrecked. That night he boarded a work train carrying a crew of men making repairs and got as far as East Sandwich, where he was stopped by a washout. Leaving the train, he waded three miles through drifts to Sandwich where he hired a man to drive him to Buzzards Bay and boarded a train for Boston. He got there with the news on Tuesday morning.

But he had no details. These were supplied in part on Tuesday night by Harry Sparrow, storekeeper at Orleans. He had received the news from a fisherman who had gathered some of the debris. Making a trip as devious as the one Mr. Ward had made, he drove forty miles through snowdrifts to get to Boston, arriving Tuesday night. Other details were supplied by the *Dallas*, arriving soon afterward, bringing some of the wreckage — a life belt, a piece of a stateroom door with the knob still on it, and the cornice from the *Portland*'s cabin.

As soon as he received the news, Mr. Williams, agent of the line, had set out on a tug, accompanied by reporters, for Cape Cod. By this time twenty bodies had been recovered and lay in the establishments of local undertakers as well as in temporary morgues that had been set up, one in a blacksmith shop, one in a railroad station. He was able to identify some members of the crew. Relatives following, having reached the Cape by one hazardous way or another, went from village to village, sometimes on foot through drifts, to view the victims. A few, among them Mr. Freeman and Mr. Flower, were identified at once. To assist in the identification of others, the papers printed their descriptions:

> A man, 45 years, 170 lbs. 5 ft. 8 in. light complexion, sandy moustache. Fully dressed. No papers for identity. Clothes of fine material. Black suit, cutaway coat, heavy tan shoes with mark *Just Wright*. White collar. Laundry mark 6019. Lavender tie, new cuffs, gray mixed undershirt, bluish gray silk stockings. Overcoat black, of fine material, with a half satin back. Absolutely nothing in his pockets.

> A man, thought to be William Mosher, of Gorham, 25 years old, well-dressed in black suit, red leather shoes, light necktie and broadcloth overcoat. Silk handkerchief, initial M. Peculiar gold watch of foreign make. Plain gold ring. Money in pocket and 2 seat checks to theatre Friday night.

> A girl, 20 years. Blue eyes, dark brown hair. Full set of teeth. Little finger right hand a ring — stone washed away. Side setting of ring was of pearls.

> A man, well dressed in a black suit and overcoat, wearing a white shirt, with opal studs set in gold. He had russet shoes. Was of the blonde type, with light hair and moustache, and in his pockets were a gold watch,

145

$2 in cash, a stateroom key, "No. 75," and two handker-chiefs, one of which was marked "W." On one finger was a gold ring. Wore a blue necktie. He was five feet, 9 inches tall, and weighed 150 pounds.

A man, well and completely dressed in brown checked suit and black overcoat. 37–38 years, 5 ft. 6 in., 150 lbs. Underclothing was of finest make. All could be found in pocket was small pocket comb and knife.

A woman about 30 years of age. She had on no clothing except one shoe.

A mulatto girl, 20 years old, weight 115 pounds, 5 ft. 3 in. Probably one of the waitresses and possibly the daughter of one of the stewardesses. The body was partially dressed and had on a plaid cape. There was an opal ring on third finger of left hand. Hair remarkably long and thick.

A man with brown hair and reddish moustache; height, 5 ft. 10 in. Weight about 160 lbs. Very well dressed. Gold watch and chain, stand-up collar and blue tie. A plain gold ring on third finger of left hand, having initials of M.L.B. on the inside.

A woman about 45 years old, dressed in night-gown, shoes and stockings. 180 lbs., 5 ft. 9 in. Hair dark, streaked with gray. On finger a ring with the words Forget-Me-Not.

A girl about 18 or 20 with a tiny gold watch and chain entangled in her flowing hair.

It was December 22 before the last body ever to be found was washed ashore. Though the passenger list was never reliably determined, it is probable that between 140 and 190 persons had gone down.

As soon as the initial shock was over, all along the coast people began to ask questions. Just what had happened? Everyone who knew the sea had his theory. But most people, including the officials at the Lifesaving Station, accepted Mr. Williams's explanation.

> I am sure that the *Portland* foundered at sea . . . where or how the wreck occurred I do not think will ever be known. My opinion is that she was first caught in the heavy seas near Thatcher's Island and that she went down somewhere between there and the Cape. Her guards and paddle-boxes must have been smashed by the heavy seas, and although she was a staunch boat, as her class goes, she could not stand the wrenching and pounding of the waves. Everything above the main deck — all the deck houses — I believe was torn away. With the steamer bare above the deck and the hull smashed and leaking, it seems to me that she must have plunged down, carrying every soul on board with her.

There was another question, the one more frequently asked. Whose fault is it? Just who is responsible? Mr. Liscomb, manager of the line, placed the blame on Captain Blanchard, issuing the following statement:

> It was clearly a case of bad judgment and disobedience of orders on the part of Capt. Blanchard. Every day about 3 P.M. we have a special weather report from N.Y. by wire and before the steamer starts each night the N.Y. report is compared with those of Boston and Portland and then it is decided whether the boat shall sail. Our motto has always been to err on the safe side and, in fact, I have heard that people have sometimes referred to us as the "Old Granny" line, because we would not sail in threatening weather. We never allow a boat to go out in a gale or a snow storm and if they get caught after they are getting to sea they are instructed to return.
> Probably half a dozen times during the winter,

on an average, we miss a trip entirely, owing to our cautiousness in case of storms, so you see, in directing that the *Portland* be kept in port last Saturday, I was simply following the usual policy.

On Monday Mr. Williams informed me that he had delivered to Capt. Blanchard my instructions not to sail. Once before when I told Capt. Blanchard to remain in port for a few hours on account of threatening weather, he demurred, and expressed ability to "get there all right," but I insisted and he complied with my wishes.

He was evidently convinced that the approaching storm was not going to be very severe, perhaps founding that belief on the prediction which I believe was in Saturday's Government report that the wind on Sunday would be northwest.

The watchman on the wharf tells me that when the boat sailed the Captain said to him, "Keep an eye out for me. I may come back," showing that he did expect rough weather and knew what to do when he encountered it.

At first others also blamed the captain. There were two stories current about him, both relating to Captain Dennison of the *Bay State*. One claimed that in their telephone conversation on Saturday, Captain Blanchard had brushed off Captain Dennison's warning by stating that he would be in Portland Sunday night for reasons of his own. The other story suggested what those reasons were: It said that Captain Blanchard had expected to command the *Bay State*, the new boat on the line, and resented that the position had been given to Captain Dennison, the youngest captain in the service, whom everyone called the Kid Pilot. Hearing that the *Bay State* was to be kept in Portland that night, he had decided, so the story went, to sail proudly into Portland Harbor on Sunday morning, thus showing his superior seamanship.

But those who used their heads were asking another

question: If Captain Blanchard had been forbidden to sail, why did Mr. Williams allow him to go? Reporters pressed officials for an explanation:

"Mr. Williams, how did you as agent of your company, permit the *Portland* to sail?"

"We have nothing to say on that point," Mr. Williams replied.

"Then you decline to answer the question?"

"No, we don't decline to answer anything," interposed J.L. Liscomb, the general manager of the company, "We do not wish to put it that way."

Again Mr. Williams was asked:

"How did you, as agent of the company, having delivered the order of Manager Liscomb to Capt. Blanchard that he should not sail, permit him to leave at all?"

"Why, he often went out and came back again," Mr. Williams replied. "That did not appear to be any worse night than a good many others on which he had been out and returned."

"You gave him the order that he was not to go?"

"Yes."

"And you were the agent of the company? Is the captain superior to the agent?"

"He was the captain, and he took the responsibility. He knew his orders."

"We can't talk any more on this matter," interposed Mr. Liscomb. "We have said all that is necessary."

You sat in your office and gave Capt. Blanchard manager Liscomb's orders?" was asked agent Williams.

"Yes, I did," answered the agent.

Manager Liscomb said that he had no doubt that the captain received the order. "The captain had charge of the boat; he had a United States license," added the manager.

"But this captain was sailing away with your property, which you didn't want him to do. You had ordered him not to go, and Mr. Williams, your agent, representing your interests, gave him your order not to go, and yet he permitted him to go."

To this Mr. Liscomb made no reply.

Sympathy had begun to swing toward Captain Blanchard. On December 5 the *Boston Transcript* carried this story:

> It is the general opinion among the residents and old mariners on Cape Cod that Capt. Blanchard never left port without orders, or at least against direct orders from the agent of the company. It is not the custom of captains of vessels to go against the orders of their superiors, especially in a case of this kind, and for that reason they believe that Capt. Blanchard, a dead man, has been unjustly condemned for the loss of his ship.

The same day Representative Fitzgerald introduced a resolution in the House, asking an investigation. On December 6 Dr. Joshua Lewis, chairman of the State Board of Charity, criticized the steamship company for making no effort to patrol the beaches, looking for bodies, which he believed came in, and, unnoticed, immediately washed out again. Backed by Dr. Davis, the State Medical Examiner, he suggested that a small steamer be chartered to patrol the area.

Meanwhile the Governor himself had instigated a search, sending out the tug *Harold*, under the direction of the State Police. For a week it searched, traveling 400 miles, and found nothing. At the same time the United States government sent out an expedition with divers, in an attempt to locate the hull of the *Portland* believing that most of the bodies would be found within it. A few days later the *Boston Globe* concentrated a search in the area of Peaked Hill Bar, dragging a long chain between two tugs, proving to the satisfaction of its organizers that the *Portland* did not sink there.

150

As a result of these expeditions, there were two new theories. One had it that the *Portland* had collided with another ship, possibly the *King Philip*, whose wreckage was beginning to come in. Another suggested the *Portland* might have tangled with the Anglo-American cable broken in that area on the night of the storm.

Relatives of the dead, disinterested in theories, had already begun to talk of legal action. By December 27 two suits had been filed. On that same day attorneys for the steamship company filed a petition in the United States District Court requesting the court to pronounce that the disaster had occurred "by Act of God and perils of the sea," and without fault on their part. The Court complied.

For weeks afterward some wreckage kept coming in, a little here, a little there — making in all, from the entire steamer, "only about half a dozen horse loads," as one farmer on the Cape put it. And now and then over the years a fisherman, dredging, has brought up something — a brass lantern, a chandelier, a few keys. But nothing has been added to the story of that fateful night.

It is a story no New Englander will ever forget.

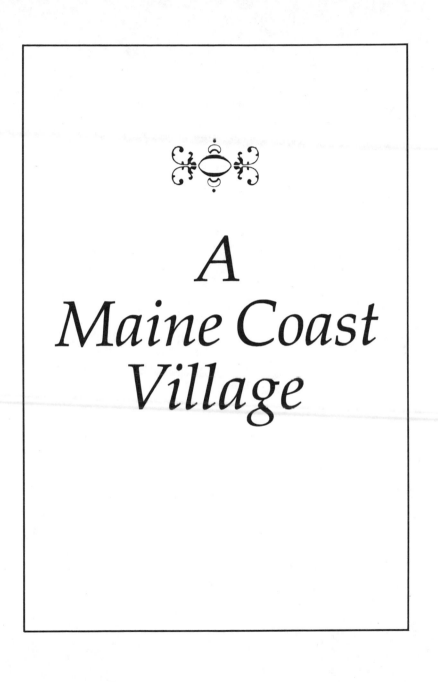

A
Maine Coast
Village

A Maine Coast Village

he chapters that follow present a unique and human history of the Maine coast in the eighteenth and nineteenth centuries. They portray a representative Maine village and the people who shaped it. The village is Edgecomb.

Among the stories are those of Samuel Trask, founder of Edgecomb, who for many years was a captive of the Indians; of Moses Davis, coffinmaker, magistrate, and tea fancier, who kept a diary for almost half a century in which he recorded local illnesses, accidents, lawsuits; of Stephen Parsons, one of Maine's first efficiency experts; and of Fanny Stone, postmaster for forty-seven years.

These stories show the village itself — its school, its early library, its general store. They also show the experiences of its people at sea, including mutiny.

This is not a conventional history. Rather it is a lively and colorful one, presenting with astonishing accuracy the spirit of Maine's coast.

M.S.

Samuel Trask

t was some time early in the eighteenth century that Samuel Trask first saw the Sheepscot. It was a beautiful river, indented with coves and bordered with marshes beyond which great forests stretched. Free of shoals, it abounded in islands — some mere ledges, stained white by the sea birds; some larger, crusted with just enough soil to feed sweet fern and juniper; a few, topped with pine and spruces.

It was a river vibrant with life. The winds seldom left it. Gulls wheeled above it. Crows crossed it noisily. Geese, migrating, followed it. Ducks darkened the sky above its marshes, and eagles sought out the tallest trees along its shore. Fish — salmon, smelt, shad — swarmed its waters. Seals sunned on its ledges, and whales cruised leisurely near its mouth.

Samuel Trask found a river already rich in history. Primitive man knew it and left his records in the great heaps of shells, whitened by time and weather, that still lie along its shore. The Wawenock Indians knew it. A simple, dignified people, they had lived from the river and from its banks. They had fished, dug clams, dredged for oysters and scallops; they had caught the giant lobsters. They had hunted the seal and the whale, gathered the eggs of sea birds and shot the fowl that nested in the marshes. In the woods they had tracked the deer and the moose, trapped the bear and the beaver.

Early explorers knew the river's mouth. Cabot, Verrazano, Gomez were certainly among them, and probably Jean Allefonsce, who, in 1527 claimed to have found, somewhere between Nova Scotia on the north and New England on the south, a fabulous province called Norumbega, containing "a faire town and a great river abounding in fish." Fanned by his stories, Champlain set out to find it and in his search sailed up the river itself, stopping at what is now Wiscasset and then passing through Hell Gate to the Kennebec.

But this was in 1604. By the time Samuel Trask came, trading was already established, for if the New World had neither gold nor silver to offer, it had riches of another sort. For more than a century, ships had been coming from England and the coastal countries of Europe seeking fish — the great haddock and cod — seeking furs, and sassafras for the plague and scurvy. First the trading had been carried on in small boats and canoes. Then stations were set up along the river bank. Among the earliest of these was one started in 1623 by Christopher Leavitt, friend of Samoset, on Cape Newagen. Soon there were nine such stations along the Sheepscot. One of the largest operated in the early 1650s near Arrowsic. Valued at twenty thousand pounds, it was built around a fort, for its protection. A complete settlement, it had saw and grist mills, bake houses, blacksmith and cooper shops. A shipyard was nearby.

Samuel Trask saw a hardy, stable race. It had not

always been so. In 1625 the inhabitants had been described as "strangers, speculators, transients, with considerable admixture of sea-faring adventurers" — men who "cut one another's throat for beaver." But hardship had matured them. For fifty years they had endured Indian warfare.

Cheated and betrayed to the point of violence, the Indians had stolen cattle, burned houses, mills, barns, captured and murdered as was their whim. At first they had had the advantage, for they far outnumbered the settlers. They had no houses or barns to lose. They were used to fatigue and acclimated to cold and wilderness.

At each attack some of the settlers had fled to the garrisons, some to the islands. But always some returned and started in again. These were the people Samuel Trask saw.

He came at a time of peace. Confident that the wars were over, the settlers were attempting to set up laws for government. Had he been a man, and a free one, Samuel Trask would perhaps have stayed at the time, but he was a boy and a captive as well. He was to remain a captive until he was twenty-two years old. Then he was to return to the Sheepscot and found a settlement, where, through cold, drought, fire, flood, earthquake, famine, war, he was to live out his long and eventful life.

Samuel Trask was born in Salem in 1703 of superior and spirited stock. His great-grandfather, Captain William Trask, was one of the "Old Planters" of Salem and a color-bearer in Captain Endecott's company. He was several times a selectman and from 1635 to 1639 served as a representative from Salem to the General Court of Massachusetts. In 1637 he commanded an expedition against the Pequod Indians and as a result "signalized himself and won the gratitude of his country." He was to Salem what Miles Standish was to the Plymouth colony.

His son, John, though less colorful, was also a vigorous man and prominent in the community, being at one time a selectman and at another a constable. Both were millers. John's son, Elias, father of Samuel, was a blacksmith and, like his forebears, virile. He married three times and raised three families.

Samuel Trask, even as a boy, was Captain William all over again — bold, fiery, daring. In 1711, while playing in the forest where children were forbidden to go, he was captured by the Indians. Since he was by far their most outstanding child, the family was distraught. Assisted by the neighbors, they searched the forest while the militia dragged the nearby river and scoured the marsh. For weeks the search continued, but no trace of the missing boy was found.

Remembering, no doubt, the services of Captain William, the town appropriated a sum of money for the boy's ransom. But the ransom was never paid, for the years failed to reveal even a clue to his whereabouts. Finally in 1725 the money was used toward the purchase of a town bell.

It is not strange that the boy could not be found, for, following his capture, he was taken to Maine, on the Penobscot River, near the domain of Jean Vincent, Baron De St. Castin, a French nobleman, who had adopted the life of the Indians, married the daughter of one of their chiefs, and equipped them for war against the English.

Here the boy showed great skill as a huntsman. Some years after his capture, during a famine when the only subsistence came from the cranberry bogs, he, in the presence of Castin's second son, Joseph, proved better than the Indians themselves in shooting wild geese that flew over. Delighted, Castin purchased him for ten pistoles (about forty dollars) and put him to work on board his sloop. There are no records to tell how old he was at the time, but he stayed with Castin until 1725, when the sloop was captured by an English privateer.

After fourteen years of captivity — not all unhappy, one fancies — Samuel Trask was free again.

A legend that Trask, following his release from Castin, was associated with Captain Kidd is clearly false, for Kidd was hanged in 1702, a year before Samuel's birth. Instead, he was kept as a pilot by the English until a treaty was made by them and the Indians in 1727.

There is nothing to show where he was in the years immediately following, but in 1730 he was back in Salem. It could not have been a happy homecoming. His mother was dead, and so were his grandparents. His father had remarried. The family had by this time lost its prestige as well as its prosperity. Salem was by no means the village he remembered.

He did not stay long, only long enough to have courted and married Hannah Stuart (also spelled Stewart) of Rowley. Right afterward, he started with her back to Maine. Their son, Samuel Junior, was, according to Maine records, born on the Sheepscot the following year. Then something — perhaps responsibilities in Hannah's family — took them back again to Rowley.

In 1737, having sold Hannah's property there for 140 pounds, they returned to Maine. It was a time of peace. Trade was progressing. New settlers, notably Scotch-Irish, were coming. Exactly where they lived with their rapidly growing family, ultimately eight sons and a daughter, is not known, though it was in the vicinity of Wiscasset. But a deposition recorded by Samuel before a Judge on May 31, 1789, casts some light upon his early activities.

> I, Samuel Trask, aged more than eighty years, have lived in Sheepscutt River more than 48 years and in my first settlement there I was well acquainted with the Indians and well understood their language, as in my younger days I was captivated by them and lived among them and frequently went up and down said river in canoes, rafts and vessels. The Indians at that time used frequently to be and lodge in my house in numbers.

The peace was not a complete one. As new settlers came, working inland, the Indians grew more restive, for they had insisted from the first that the white man could live only as far as the salt water flowed. Barns were burned again, livestock destroyed, homes pillaged. Every town had its garrison and its militia. No man worked in his field without a guard.

In 1745 came the battle for Louisburg, French capital of the East, a fortress on Cape Breton Island that had taken twenty-five years to build, with an eight-foot moat, walls thirty feet high and, at their base, forty feet thick. It was, moreover, armed with formidable batteries and manned by two thousand veteran soldiers. Against this supposedly impregnable fortress marched a volunteer American army of four thousand rookies — farmers, fishermen, artisans and shopkeepers — led by Sir William Pepperrell, almost as untrained as they were. Samuel Trask was among them, as a member of Dalrymple's Company, Preble's regiment.

The attack had color and vigor and drama — all the things that he loved well. It had, moreover, all the qualities of a crusade. Apart from the fact that the colonists wanted to protect their trade and their fisheries, they were concerned about the hold of Popery on their shores. All Protestants, the attackers included a good many preachers. One was the Reverend Samuel Moody of York, of whom John Adams wrote to Abigail: "He has an ascendency and authority over the people here, as absolute as that of any prince in Europe, not excepting his holiness." Parson Moody carried a hatchet with him to break up religious images. Also, there was the Reverend Moses Coffin of Newbury, who doubled as a drummer, and whose Bible shielded his heart from a bullet during the siege. Beneath a banner bearing the words *Nil Desperandum Christo Duce*, with only sixty ships, including one frigate and a few armed sloops, and with very little ammunition, they made the assault and won one of the most astonishing victories in American history.

There are stories, and probably true ones, of Samuel Trask's activities there. He was, they say, in the foreground, unloading the powder casks, carrying them high through the surf on head and shoulders; dragging the guns over more than two miles of roadless terrain; hauling them through sucking mud; hacking the forest; setting the batteries in position, all the time facing enemy fire; hoisting the cannon a mile and a quarter over almost inaccessible cliffs, sleeping without a shelter through the cold, foggy nights; weakened, like a third of the others, by fever and dysentery.

He must have been there at the moment of victory while Parson Moody wielded his axe, and Pepperrell, seeing the full strength of the fortress cried, "God has been with us." He must have heard the music from the same fifes and drums that were to rally the patriots at Lexington.

He was not to hear them again. It was his last military battle.

But ahead lay battles of another sort. Not long after Samuel Trask returned from Louisburg, he with about three hundred others established a new settlement "in several places" on the east side of the Sheepscot. One of these places was on the shore of a wide, sheltered basin, later called "The Eddy," where the tides pressed through a gorge between the point of Jeremy Squam and Folly Islands, now called Westport and Davis Islands. Another was on the shores of the cove later called Mill Cove. By water (there were, of course, no roads) the distance between the settlements was only about eleven miles. The settlers bought the land from one John Mason, who, in turn, had bought it in 1652 from the Indian Sagamores Robinhood, Dick Swash, and Jack Pudding.

Settlers along the river had always known hardship. The weather had been against them; season after season had brought extremes. In 1697 there was a famine, during which "some, eating dogs and cats, died horribly famished." In 1729 there was a terrific earthquake. "Beasts ran howling to the fields in great distress. The houses rocked and creaked. Chimneys were riven. Doors, windows and walls were broken; the glass was shattered and, in some instances, fell to the floors. All nature was in commotion. Men, with surprise and terror, trembling with the earth, on land and on sea, tossed with their ship."

Such disasters were to return. In 1749 and 1750 grasshoppers descended. "No vegetables escaped these greedy troops, they even devoured the potato tops." In the spring of 1756 "worms in armies and in millions" covered the countryside, "threatening to devour everything green." In August 1760 a hurricane leveled "houses, barns, trees, cows, and almost every other thing, bleakly exposed." In 1763 there was a "great freshet, with waters higher than ever before in recollection of anyone living." In 1764 frost came in the middle of June, nipping the corn crop.

But perhaps no years took greater endurance than 1754 and 1755. The winter was excessively cold. Forests were drifted and clam flats were frozen solid. People lived on frost-fish, buttermilk, and, when they could get them, roasted potatoes. A man had to work all day for enough money to buy a quart of meal. The Indians, disregarding the pledges given their chiefs, still marauded.

So great was their distress that in 1755 some four hundred settlers in the area signed their names or made their marks (about 20 percent were illiterate) upon a petition, written with remarkable restraint, to the Governor of Massachusetts, asking assistance. Samuel Trask and his son, Samuel Junior, were among them. In part the petition read:

> . . . Settlers by reason of their situation and present weak state are exposed to the Indians and in a defenseless condition against their hostilities, and the precariousness of Indian Peace gives such just apprehension of Danger as extreamly discourages your Petitioners in their business and must tend to detur others from settling with them . . . pray that some measures may be by your wisdom made for their Safeguard and Defense.
> April 22, 1755.

At this time they experienced another kind of hardship. For ten years now, to first one settlement and then another, imposters had appeared, calling themselves Proprietors, and, pretending to hold deeds from the Indians, claimed the land which had been cleared at so great a cost. For a long time they had plagued Wiscasset. Then in 1754 such a group came to the settlement on the east of the river, and began to lay out lots.

The settlers were in despair. Even Samuel Trask was helpless. In law-abiding communities you couldn't drive off men with muskets, especially where those men had muskets, too, and deeds of a kind as well. What they needed was a lawyer to plead their case. There were no lawyers on the frontier.

Just when it looked as if all were lost, a Boston lawyer by the name of Kent heard of their plight and offered to defend them without charge. How he did it there are no records to tell, but he saved them, and in their relief and gratitude they named the settlement Freetown. In 1774 it was incorporated and renamed Edgecombe (later spelled Edgecomb) in honor of Lord Edgecomb who had shown sympathy for the American colonies.

Here at the Eddy, Samuel Trask lived out his long life. He earned his livelihood, like his grandfather and great-grandfather, by running a mill, assisted for a time by his son Samuel Junior. He was more than the founder of the town. He was its patriarch. He handled all affairs with the Indians, and, being as crafty as they were, he handled them well. He was recognized as the best guide in the area. Because of his skill with herbs — a skill he had learned from the Indians — he became a medical authority, being known generally as Dr. Trask.

He himself seldom knew illness, and, according to legend often scoffed but supported by no less an authority than the *New England Historical and Genealogical Register*, he lived to the age of 118 years. According to testimony of his descendants, "he walked a mile home and back on the day of his death, ate his dinner, sat back, appeared to be failing, and soon died."

166

His life had been rich in experience. He had known captivity and freedom, war and peace, scarcity and plenty. He had known the mores of two races. He had seen land devastated and then grow green, villages destroyed and soon built up again. He had seen the wilderness give way to farm land, barter to foreign trade. He had fathered nine children, and his descendants — most of them sturdy and long-lived — people an entire region.

His was, indeed, a full and extraordinary life.

Moses Davis

n the west side of Davis Island, near a bend in the Sheepscot, lies a small family graveyard shaded by locust trees. In it stands a gathering of stones, rain-streaked and covered with lichen. One of them marks the grave of Moses Davis.

A modest slate stone, it bears this modest epitaph:

Early devoted to Christ, one of the first settlers and respected fathers of this town, he lived and died in the faith and hope of the Gospel.

But for one thing, the man who lies beneath it might today be forgotten. This is a diary — human, spontaneous — which he began in 1772 and kept almost daily, with the exception of the years between 1777 and 1781, until a few months before his death in 1824.

Of Welsh descent, Moses Davis was born in Hampton Falls, New Hampshire, on September 23, 1743. When he was five years old, he was taken to Boston where he attended school until he was fourteen. Then he was apprenticed to Captain Onesiphorus Tileston to learn the trade of housewright. He lived in Boston until he was twenty-one when he moved to Newburyport. There, in 1766, "on a very bright Moon Shining night," he married Sarah Rolfe. In 1770, already the father of three children, he moved his family to Edgecomb, then called Fieetown, and settled on Folly Island that now bears his name.

He was, indeed, a man of many parts. By necessity he was a farmer. His crops consisted largely of corn, rye, cabbage, parsnips, turnips and potatoes. In 1791 he shipped forty bushels of potatoes by schooner to Virginia to purchase flour or corn. In 1814 when his farm prospered, he harvested 144 bushels of large eatable ones and twenty-five bushels to feed his hogs. He also raised a few sheep, killing their ticks by a wash of "Cambury and tobacco." He did not shear them himself, but hired it done for five cents a sheep.

As a farmer, he had, of course, an eye for the weather. "Clear and cold," he might record. Or, "Small wind and pleasant morning." Or, merely, "a very warm day." In the winter, when he had more leisure, his observations lengthened.

> Thursday, March 31 1785 — The snow is now five feet in the woods and all blocked up in the clard land more than ever was known for this time of year — the roads are all Block up so that is no stiring to do any business — and hay very scarce in general.
>
> Wednesday March 31 1790 — Cool and wind N.W. blows fresh — this has been a very difficult month, the snow is very deep in the clear land — & has been blocked up this fortnight, but little Passing — a great famine seems to prevail throughout this County.

For him, things happened less by the clock than by the sky and tide. His wife returned "Just at dusk." His friend Captain Decker died "Just at Sunset." He arrived home "at Candle light." His daughter Huldah gave birth to a child "at two hours flood." Mrs. Pearson of Wiscasset died, "the sun about an hour high afternoon."

By trade he was a carpenter. Hardly a week passed without his recording something he had made — a ladder, a bedstead, a table, a trundlebed, a boat, a cheese press, a chest of drawers, a meal chest, a sleigh. He built a number of dwellings in Edgecomb, among them what is now called the Marie Antoinette house, the schoolhouse, and the meeting house. But the greatest demand on his skill lay in the making of coffins, in which he was sometimes assisted by his son, Moses, Jr.

Life was precarious along the river. Until the time there were roads, it was the only thoroughfare. Drownings were frequent; deaths by accident, commonplace. Joshua Sawyer died "by means of a mortal cut in the ancle." John Chase "fell off his horse and killed himself." David Gove died from "a fall from a cart." William Trask "died from a wound in his thigh."

Sickness was constant. Most dreaded was smallpox.

Sunday August 25 1793 — Went down to James Chase in company with Mr. Sears and moved Mrs. Sweatt & her daughter to the Pest house to have the small pox — afternoon came back and sent Moses down with some things for Mrs. Sweatt —

Monday August 26 1793 — Went early this morning to Winthrop Dodges and moved Thomas Sweatt to the Pest house who has the Small pox — afternoon worked on meeting house Self & Moses —

Saturday August 31 1793 — Went to see Mr. Asa Goves & to the other house of small pox to see what was wanting & came back home and heard that Mr.

Trask had provided things for them — I sent them some herbs and Taminind.

Monday September 2 1793 — Went to help bury Mr. Asa Gove who died last night with the small pox buryd him on his own land — smoaked myself & returned to the meeting house to work about 5 o'clock—

Of the number of coffins he made, Moses Davis kept no count, but there must have been hundreds. This entry is typical:

Saturday July 14 1804 — Moses & Mr. Merrill made Mr. Chapman's coffin (Mr. Chapman was the minister). Self went to Wiscasset in the forenoon & bought the furniture for sd Coffin etc. Afternoon fixed blacking and blacked the Coffin. Moses & Mr. Merrill carried it up and put Mr. Chapman in etc.

He seems not only to have made the coffins, but to have assumed other responsibilities relating to death.

Wednesday March 6 1793 — Afternoon went to Nath Goves & to Mr. Hoods & returned with the Corps of Mrs. Trask who died this morning at Mr. Merrills — helpd the Corps into the house and agreed to watch with her the night.

Monday January 6 1794 — Went to Wiscasset in order to get burying cloth (rented for 2 shillings) and engaged Mr. Moore to preach a funeral sermon.

Tuesday December 18 1792— Made Capt. Deckers coffin —

Wednesday Decembere 19 1792 — Went to Widow Deckers & assisted her to get ready for the funeral — Mrs. Davis assisting also —

Thursday December 20 1792 — Went to Widow Deckers & fixd matters for the funeral, about 2 o'clock intered Captain Decker — taried with Mrs. Decker till about 9 o'clock in the evening and then came home with Mrs. Davis.

By experience he was a surveyor and laid out most of the early roads. He must have worked with dispatch.

> Fryday September 21 1787 — Run out the Road acrost the woods to Damariscotta & then went to Boothbay line and run the Road to Mr. Rings at Newcastle line & returned as far as Mr. Dodges.
>
> Saturday September 22 1787 — Run the road from Sol Gove field to Boothbay line and then over to James Chase & run from the Cross Point to Mr. Cliffords where we left off & finished the whole.

Whatever he did he had a sharp eye for profit, always being ready to make an honest dollar. Until 1785, anyone wishing to go to Wiscasset on foot or horseback had to go by way of Alna, a journey of about five miles. He saw the possibility of cutting that distance by a ferry across the Sheepscot, and that year petitioned the Court of Session for the right to run one. The ferry, a scow propelled by sculling, took its first passenger on Wednesday, June 15. Business was good. In 1793 it carried fifty-six horses and two hundred men. Moses Davis himself ran it until January, 1811, when he turned it over to his son, Moses, Jr.

He owned a fishing boat. "Went to Wiscasset," he wrote, "and bought a fishing boat of Saml Brier agreed and gave note for 200 dollars for her. Took out new papers for her in my name and put Silvester Pierce Master of her. Pierce went down river in order for fishing." Three weeks later Pierce returned with a good catch of "Herren." So successful was the arrangement that the next spring Mr. Pierce took the boat out for the season.

When he had surplus money he loaned it. "Went to Wiscasset & met Nathan Adams," he wrote, "and let him have 200 dollars and he mortgaged his farm to me for the same, to be paid in three years from the Date with interest and also agreed to give me a good clock in the bargain to be delivered on demand., (This clock is still in the possession of the Davis family and is still running.)

Most of his life he held some public office. He was the first town clerk, keeping the records for eight years. He served one year as town treasurer, and nineteen years, though not consecutively, on the Board of Selectmen, where his annual salary was approximately three pounds. In 1788 he was elected delegate to the Constitutional Convention, at which Massachusetts ratified the Constitution of the United States. He records nothing of the Convention itself. His only entry reads thus:

> Thursday February 14 1788 — After attending the Convention in Boston 30 days Returned home this afternoon about sunset very much fatigued with my journey.

For forty-eight years he was Justice of the Peace. During these years, as "Squire Davis," he not only performed 183 marriages but held court regularly in Whittier's Tavern in Wiscasset as well. A representative selection of his cases follows:

> Wednesday August 13 1783 — Daniel Leeman once bound to Moses Davis came here and I granted him a warrant against Allen Malcolm for striking him.
> Tuesday November 6 1787 — Went before Day with Mr. Dan Websters to his house and wrote a warrant against Isaac Farnsworth for Begetting a Child by & with Mary Webster —
> Tuesday May 3 1791 — David Cargill came before me and made complaint against himself for breach of the peace in kicking Rob't Cochran in the back side and paid a fine of five shillings for the same.

He seems to have been tolerant of those who were brought before him, so tolerant, indeed, that once he subjected himself to public criticism. It is interesting to note, however, than when his mind was made up, he did not change it.

> Tuesday July 29 1806 — Wrote a letter to Sebra Crooker to come and pay his fine for breach of Sabbath & by desire of Mr. Fly.
>
> Saturday September 6 1806 — Mr. Fly brought in a comp t ag t me for not prosecuting Sebra Crooker for breach of Sabbath agreeable to his compt & the Ch h concluded that I was to blame, I therefore made such a confession as I could conscientously do, but it did not give satisfaction to the church & so the matter stands unsettled —
>
> Thursday September 18 1806 — Mr Sewall was here this forenoon and we had some conversation with him about church matters relative Mr. Fly & myself but settled nothing —
>
> Monday September 22 1806 — Deacon Ring & Mr. Dan'l Hood came to see the matter Mr. Fly laid before the church relative my not prosecuting Sebra Crooker by Fly comp't — conversed on the subject & concluded to let the matter stand for further consideration.
>
> Thursday September 25 1806 — Mr. Fly came here & Mr. Hood & Mr. Adama and settled the dispute between Mr. Fly & myself relative Sebra Crooker breaking the Sabbath & by burying all matters and to say no more about the matter & to be friendly hereafter.

A lover of peace himself, he often closed a case with an exhortation to both parties to forget all rancor.

With all his other activities, he found time to carry the mail. Until 1788 there had been no regular mail service to Wiscasset. Letters, papers and parcels were brought in by vessels. That year bridle paths opened, and a post-rider came first fortnightly, then weekly, from Portland. In 1790 a post office was opened in Wiscasset, the easternmost one in the United States. There mail was received, adver-

174

tised, and held for people who lived beyond. In 1805 Moses Davis opened the route to Boothbay. How often he went is not clear, but his annual pay was twenty-one dollars.

Though he worked hard, he was no ascetic. When times were good, he set a good table. Plain food was not enough. "M. Dodge went away with Capt. Patterson for Boston," he wrote. "I sent 10 dollars for a barrel of superfine flour." He always had plenty of drink at his house. "Halld home my cider from David Trasks. Made thirteen barrels," he wrote. "Brought home a Barrell sugar & 3½ Gallons Rum," he wrote again. Three days later he added, "Went this morning to see Capt. Decker and brought home a case of Gin."

But his favorite drink was tea. Time after time he records occasions when he drank it. "Went to Wiscasset · Carried Wife and Drank tea at Major Huses." He wrote again: "Afternoon went in sleigh with Mrs. Davis to Winthrop Dodges. Drank tea there and returned home a little after sunset." Later: "Went to meeting house and Mr. Richard Merrill delivered an Oration on the Commemoration of the death of General Washington — after meeting went to Capt. Eben Gove and drank tea returned home at dusk." For his own tea he paid the enormous price of 52 cents a pound.

What he had, he shared. Seldom did his family eat alone. There were always guests coming. Sometimes they were casual guests who dropped in in the course of travel. "Capt. Tucker of Bristol here and tarried for dinner with me & we had a free conversation etc.," he wrote. Sometimes they were the men and women he married. "John Clark 2d came here with Clarisa Dodge & I married them and they stayed to supper," he wrote again. "This afternoon Mr. Dalton & Widow Moore came here and were married Just at Sundown — tarried all night," he recorded.

More often guests were relatives and friends. On

Thanksgiving 1807, he wrote, "Wm Clifford & wife & children & Jane Woodbridge & brother & Henry Dodge & wife & child & Morris Dodge & wife & children & Daniel Dodge & Moses Davis & wife dined here." His hospitality was not limited to his table. On July 13, 1793, he wrote, "Saw Mrs. Jewett and had her to come home to my house and she would have proper care taken of her."

He liked fine clothing. When times were hard, he wore corduroy, paid for in timber, and a hat traded with Captain Wood of Wiscasset for "2 dollars in fresh meat." But in 1795 with the return of prosperity he "Paid Mr. Anderson 49 Shillings for Sattin for waistcoat and Breeches." In 1800 he "Paid Capt. Follansbee 8 dollars for a wig which he brought from Exeter." Two years later he went to Wiscasset and got trimmings for a suit of clothes. Mr. Lock, the tailor, came to make it. The next year he bought "cloth for a pair of breeches at 3 dollars a yard." Later he bought "a furr hat at $7 and a wove one at $1.15." He seems to have been interested in his wife's clothing, as well, for several times he mentions having selected material for a gown. In July 1805 he bought her not only black cambric but a pattern for making it up. He indulged her, too, in other things. In January 1808, he gave her $6.25 for "a set of Chaney" (china).

He liked good times. He enjoyed hunting, especially bird hunting. On December 26, 1772 he wrote: "Firing at geese at David Trasks Kill one and brought it home. Him roasted." A few days later he hunted again. "Went over to David Trasks and found and killed two geese. Brought one home and roasted it." He liked singing. "Mr. Sears and Self went and sung sometimes with Mr. Hood," he wrote. "Tarried in the evening till 11 o'clock & then came home in a snow storm." Except for tea drinking, no diversion is mentioned more often. Sometimes the two blended. "Went to Mr. Whiting and drank tea and then we came to Mr. Sawyers to Singing Meeting."

He liked to go sleigh riding and usually took his wife with him. Sometimes he made long journeys. On January 7, 1800 he wrote: "Set out for Capt. Cloughs this morning about half after eight with my wife and went to Freeport [thirty miles away] put up at Capt. Stockbridges — had a good time and good sleying."

He liked games. On December 26, 1783 he wrote: "Kept house & played checkers all day with Capt. Dole and Mr. Colby." He did not play cards — at least the diary makes no mention that he did — but he somehow rationalized gambling. On March 7, 1805 he wrote: "Went to Wiscasset afternoon & sent a letter & 25 dollars to Jacob Rolfe to buy tickets in the South Hadley canal lottery." Three weeks later he wrote this: "Went to Doct Adams and bought 6 quarter tickets in the Amoskeag Lottery at $5.50 per ticket $1.37½ cents per quarter."

If he sometimes indulged himself, he was also indulgent of others, including those who worked for him. "Dan'l had the canoe to go after eels," he wrote, "& tarried all day." "Saml and Joseph Perkins went in the yawl down river frollicking." "M. Davis & Dodge cuting and carrying in firewood in wood house — afternoon they all went to Wiscasset to see the Elephant."

For his time and place, he was, relatively, a learned man. He read a great deal. "Rain all day," he wrote on Saturday, January 18, 1800. "Was at home reading." But most of his reading was done on Sunday. It was largely of a religious nature. He read the *Bible, Pilgrim's Progress, Holy Wars* and *Meditations Among the Tombs*. He read tracts by Atkins and Erskine and funeral sermons by Prince and Murray. He also read the first volume of Morres *Geography*, which he borrowed from the Wiscasset Library. When he took that back, he brought home the *History of Quadrupeds*. A few weeks later he began Hunter's *Biography*. The last book he ever read was the *Times of Jesus*.

Though he wrote carelessly, he wrote well. His style was matter-of-fact.

> Tuesday August 13 1811 — I went to the funeral of General Wood as a paul bearer a large number of persons collected together to attend and see said funeral a warm day.

But often it was colored by his unique choice of words. "A small flirt of snow this night," he wrote. Again, after surveying, "perambulated the line between Boothbay and Edgecomb." His writing had a dry humor, too. Of the night one of his children was born, he wrote: "Got up about one o'clock and mustered the women." Of a sheep that died, he recorded: "I had a sheep died this morning she was very much swelled. She left a lamb behind her to shirk for a living." In whatever he wrote he was exact and exhaustive. "November 6 1729 — Work at meeting house self alone, finished the outside & locked the door, brought home my tools."

Prosperous and respected though he was, he had his tragedies. Of his nine children only two, Huldah and Moses, survived him.

178

Moses Davis himself lived to be 81. Until the last month of his life he kept busy with his farming and his carpentering, his eye open all the time for any business deal that might come up. He read, received visitors, drank tea. He devoted more time to his diary, and compiled, by public request, a history of Edgecomb.

The history has been lost, but the diary remains in the possession of his great-great-grandson, Laurence Davis. It is a rare social document, revealing not only an exceptional man, but, through his shrewd and discerning eyes, a vivid picture of his times.

Squire Parsons

tephen Parsons was the most prosperous man in Edgecomb. He had, moreover, the most distinguished ancestry. Through many generations the Parsons family had produced a large number of preachers and writers; for equally long his mother's family, the Sewalls, had run to law. Both families had left England around 1630, the Sewalls settling in and around Boston, the Parsons in western Massachusetts and Connecticut.

Soon afterward a member of each family, perhaps less intellectual than his brothers, or maybe more adventurous, had taken his wife and children and pushed into the wilderness of Maine. There, just before the Revolution, with the marriage of Josiah Parsons and Sarah Sewall, both of York, the families merged. One of the offspring was Stephen Parsons.

Born in 1778, he spend his early years in Westport Island (then called Jeremy Squam) where his father ran a farm and grist mill. He had none of the opportunitities of his cousins in Massachusetts and Connecticut. Yet he did

180

go to common school, and at the age of six could read and write. Even at that age he was ingenious mechanically and efficient in devising short cuts. He was ambitious, too.

In 1801, still in his early twenties, he came to the village of Edgecomb with a young wife — his second, the first having died in 1799 — and earned their living by surveying. Since the area was rapidly expanding, he made a good thing of this work. His ability was recognized from the start, and in 1804, when he was twenty-six years old, he was chosen not only moderator for the town meeting, but also selectman.

Being astute as well as aggressive, he kept his eyes open. In 1804 he bought a schooner, the *Diamond*. In 1805, signing the deed "Stephen Parsons, gentleman," he bought from "Nathan Gove, blacksmith," a small piece of land on Mill Cove, one of the original sites of the town, along with a "pair of mill stone, together with the irons that did belong to a single geared grist mill that used to stand on said stream." He got the mill running, and the next year purchased from Thomas Melcher the adjoining three acres, on which stood an unfinished house. He was not long in finishing it.

It was an impressive house for so young a man to own — even a "gentleman." Built on an elm-shaded knoll, with a view of both coves and of Oven's Mouth as well, it was a perfect example of Georgian architecture. It had wide windows, and its broad front door was topped with a graceful fan. Of its eight rooms, high and well-lighted, seven had fireplaces, some of which were bordered with imported tiles. On the walls of the hall and two front bedrooms were delicate, graceful stencilings, applied directly to the plaster. (Some of the original pigment, which was mixed with sour milk or buttermilk, was found in the attic.) The woodwork, done entirely by hand, had a singular beauty and dignity, especially around the fireplaces and along the winding staircase. The construction was of the best. (Even the attic was plastered.) All in all it was a suitable house for his New Hampshire wife, Margaretta Fredericka, who, as her name suggests, had about her more than a touch of elegance.

She was no provincial. Her father, Benjamin Randall, founder of the Freewill Baptists, was a man of some eminence, and until her marriage her life had been spent in an atmosphere of unusual culture. Most people in Edgecomb thought she was "stuck-up," and she probably was. Still, she was a good wife for Stephen, for she was cultivated, handsome, and ambitious. Moreover, she was willing to bear children. Eventually she had nine, three of whom died in infancy.

A few people thought Stephen was stuck-up, too. It is true that he set a high value on himself. He could hardly have done otherwise. But if he seemed aloof, it was probably because of his determination to make every minute count, to overlook no opportunity. His tidemill was already prosperous. Designed for both logs and grist, it also had machinery for filling and carding. His vessel was bringing him good returns. He had begun to buy up land. Even while his house was being built, he started a brickyard and a shipyard on the shore beyond it and, in 1806, built a variety store.

Under his development, the Cove, smaller at first than the settlement at the Eddy, outgrew it in size and activity. By 1806 it had become a busy place. The mill with its great slip was surrounded by logs and a wide, fragrant floor of sawdust, bark, slabs, and edgings. The brickyard had low sheds and long tiers of bricks, ready for burning. The shipyard was noisy with the sounds of hewing and pounding and sawing, for some vessel was always in progress — at least four were built there — its stark skeleton standing high above a great pile of chips and shavings.

182

And, of course, a wharf was just below the dam, around which boats of all sorts congregated — rowboats, canoes, fishing sloops, scows.

People were always about. Some came to buy dry goods or seeds or provisions; some brought grain to be ground or wool to be carded. Others came just because everyone else was coming. They came by boat, on horseback, or on foot down the long road that followed the shore, a hard trip in mud or snow. In spring, shouting to each other above the noise of the mill, they watched a pile of bright sawdust capping the old pile while the logs were transformed into lumber. They watched the rush of smelts and alewives, the vessels loading and unloading. In summer they hung about, trading their clams or their eggs or their vegetables. In winter they stopped in at the store for warmth on their way to hunt or trap.

Very few ever went up to the big house. Margaretta seldom asked them.

The Embargo of 1807 did not have much effect upon Stephen Parsons. Neither did the war itself. To be sure, the shipyard and the brickyard closed, and the mill operated only when someone had grain to be ground. But Stephen Parsons kept busy.

He gave a great deal of time to public affairs. From 1804 he had held one town office after another — assessor, constable, selectman. Even those who envied him voted for him. At least he had get-up-and-go, they said.

He spent time on his farm, devising new tools to save labor. He also worked on his house, among other things arranging a system by which the smoke from the kitchen fireplace could be used for curing hams. It was at this time that, encouraged no doubt by Margaretta, he began to read widely — history, biography, law. He also began to collect and write down local legends, especially those that concerned Jeremy Squam Island, where he had spent his childhood.

In 1809 he set himself up as an engineer and began to repair bridges, his biggest job being at Damariscotta. In 1810 he was appointed the first postmaster in Edgecomb. The post office was in a corner of his variety store. Here mail was held until its owner paid to redeem it. In 1811 he opened his yard briefly to build the 34-ton *Betsey*, which he himself sailed.

In 1815 the selectmen decided to survey the town. This had never been done. People knew their boundaries only by brooks, trees, stakes, and stones, or the property of others as indefinitely marked as their own. Bids were requested and Stephen Parsons submitted the lowest — four hundred fifty dollars.

It was not an easy undertaking, especially in the light of the conditions prescribed. They read thus: the town must be "correctly surveyed with each man's land or lot, respectively, run out to the acceptance of the Selectmen of said town and of said commissioners, but if not done correct the persons so undertaking forfeit the expense and shall have no pay for what is done." The town, including, of course Jeremy Squam Island, covered 15,360 acres.

In spite of the severe weather, Stephen Parsons completed his map in 1815 and the selectmen accepted it. It bore this legend:

A PLAN OF THE TOWN OF EDGECOMB

By the request of the inhabitants of the Town of Edgecomb in the county of Lincoln, I have survaid said Town and estimated each lott and laid them on this Plan by a Scale of 80 rods to an Inch and have estimated each lott on Both and put their contents on the same after making alowance for Rocks, water, sunken swamps and public highways by the best of my Skill and Judgment.

Stephen Parsons
(Sworn Surveyor for
the above purpose)

As months went by, he got to be known in the surrounding counties, and people pointed him out as he passed, riding his fine horse. Well-known men from Hallowell and Augusta stopped at his house, where Margaretta, dressed in silk, greeted them while the hired girl prepared the meal. As soon as the war was over and his industries were running again, he bought a four-wheeled carriage, the first in the town.

Meanwhile he was working for the separation of Maine from Massachusetts. The issue was an old one. It had been raised in 1785, and again in 1794, with the assertion that laws passed for the good of Massachusetts were not always for the good of sparsely settled sections like Maine. With the War of 1812 the controversy had been revived. A good many people in Maine, especially those along the coast, argued again for separation, claiming that the government had made no effort to protect them from the British. They claimed, too, that, in settling the war, Boston had allowed them to lose a third of their territory.

Of course, there were those who were against separation. Many Federalists, moved by sentiment, were loath to break the traditional tie. Some objected to the cost of a new state, saying that it would be prohibitive; others merely resented any change.

In 1816 petitions for separation were sent to the General Court, signed by a fifth of the population of the District of Maine. As a result, the Court provided for a popular vote, promising that if the majority were five to four in favor of separation, a committee would be appointed to draft a constitution.

A convention was held, and the vote was taken. It was close — 11,969 to 10,347 — but still it did not provide the necessary majority. In Edgecomb only fifty-four had voted. (A man had to have ten dollars in cash and two hundred in property in order to cast a vote.) Of these, twenty-four were for separation, thirty against it. Most of the opposition came from shippers who saw no advantage for them in a change. Again the issue rested.

In 1817, and again in 1818, Stephen Parsons was appointed a representative to the General Court at Boston. While he was away, the separation issue seethed. Rallies were held all over the state. Newspapers devoted columns of letters from irate subscribers. Edgecomb took another vote which showed that five voters had gone over to the opposition. Then Congress rearranged the customs districts so that, should Maine become a state, ships would no longer have to clear at Boston. That turned the tide. In September 1819, a committee of thirty-three was chosen to meet at Portland and draw up a constitution. Stephen Parsons was a member of it. His contribution was characteristic of him. The convention had planned to use the term "Commonwealth of Maine," but before the motion could be passed, he rose, self-assured and eloquent, calling

186

attention to the possible saving of time and energy (type then being set by hand) should the word "state" be used instead. His motion was made and carried. When he returned to Edgecomb and submitted the new constitution, it received unanimous support.

Parsons was now unquestionably the town's first citizen. He was among the first in the county, too, and easily won the election as first senator to the legislature of the new state. There he was active in making the laws. It was he who insisted that voting days should be on Monday and not on Wednesday, as had been planned. The fishermen went out at the beginning of the week, he argued, and did not return until the end.

By 1820 the effects of the war with England were almost over. Trade had to some extent revived. In 1819 Stephen Parsons had reopened his shipyard, building the 22-ton *Joanna* and the 113-ton *Mistic*. In 1821 he also built the 70-ton *Margaret*. The brickyard was open, too, and business was good at the store. Stephen Parsons was now Squire Parsons. He appeared to have everything — position, prosperity, a fine family.

Life was happy for the Parsons. They all loved nature, and from every window of the house they had a beautiful view. They loved cats, and the place was alive with them. (Stephen made a little door through the plaster in the attic so that the cats could enter and hunt mice there.) In 1825, following the death of two infants, another baby was born — Quincy Adams. One can imagine the family together, driving up the long winding road in their fine carriage. In the front seat would be the two Stephens and Margaretta, carefully gloved, holding the baby; in the back, the girls, crowded together, excited and proud of their parents, especially of their distinguished father.

For twenty years things went well. Stephen Parsons

kept his business going; he read; he surveyed; he drew; he invented gadgets. Occasionally he sailed as master on one of his ships. He continued to hold local offices, and in 1823 he was given the responsibility of organizing a local board of health. As Justice of the Peace he performed many marriages. For those bold enough to come, he performed them at his own house. It must have been quite a thing to be married there, standing before one of the great fireplaces, with Margaretta drawn in, perhaps, as a witness.

For many years Stephen Parsons had kept aloof, finding scant time for his neighbors, except where business was concerned. But gradually he grew more social. In 1837 he joined the Baptist church and became its clerk. (There is no record that Margaretta ever joined.) Soon afterwards he had a great sorrow. His son, Stephen Parsons, Junior, aged thirty-three, was lost at sea. Neither parent ever recovered from that blow. Following it, Stephen Parsons stayed more and more in his own home. He still had quite a household, for two of his daughters, Sarah and Ursula, had remained unmarried. Their mother thought no one was good enough for them, the whisper ran. But Margaretta was probably not entirely to blame. Both girls loved music and poetry — Ursula was reciting poetry when she died — and such attributes did not encourage suitors in a frontier village. Whatever the reason for their spinsterhood, they seem to have been content, for they had their adored father. He read with them, walked with them, sang with them. He dazzled them with puzzles. He taught them to play chess. What suitor could possibly have equaled him?

By 1850 great prosperity had come again. The profit on lumber was as high as 40 percent. Stephen Parsons's property at the cove was assessed at $5000, an amount, of course, far less than its value but many times that of any other property in Edgecomb. But his health was bad. Since his son's death he had lost all ambition.

In 1853 he was engaged in a lawsuit with his neighbor, Simon Huff. The members of the church demanded that the case be referred to them for settlement. When neither party would agree, both were excluded from church membership "for being in a law suit . . . contrary to the Bible and also to Church discipline." It was the only public censure Stephen Parsons had ever received.

At first he defied it. This was in 1854, the year Margaretta died. He stayed at home most of the time, cared for by his two devoted daughters. Some of his days he spent in writing local history. His style improved as he wrote, and eventually became one that would have done credit to any Parsons or Sewall of any generation.

In 1856, reluctant to depend upon a will, he decided to settle some of his affairs during his own lifetime, "selling for $200" to his daughter Ursula the following:

> One piano forte $20.00, one terresterral globe $7.00, 5 mirrors $5.00, one mahogany and 2 common tables $7.00, one sofa $4.00, 2 rocking and other chairs $4.00, 4 feather beds, bedstead and bedding $20.00, 1 clock $3.00, crockery and glassware $10.00, 2 carpets $8.00, window curtains $5.00, library $10.00, desk and secretary $4.00, cooking stove and ironware $10.00, brass fire set $5.00, 12 prs. sheep marked as recorded on town record $48.00, one cow $30.00, and all other articles of household furniture not mentioned in the above schedule.

That done, he turned his mind to making peace with his God. In January 1858, a humbled Stephen Parsons presented a petition for reconsideration of his exclusion from the church.

The first vote was against him. A week later another

was taken. No record appears of it, but it is apparent that he was eventually readmitted since his name appeared again on the list of members at a later date.

He died on April 7, 1862, and lies with Margaretta and their three infants in a lovely family graveyard below the house, marked by four tall spruces. On his stone, placed there no doubt by his devoted daughters, are these words:

MARK THE PERFECT MAN

Mutiny

t happened during a gale in the middle of the Atlantic. The year was 1875. The ship was the *Jefferson Borden*, a three-masted schooner of about 600 tons, ill-fated from the day of her launching in Kennebunk in 1867. After a series of minor disasters, she was beached on the coast of Florida in 1870, so badly damaged that only her hull was salvaged. Reconditioned, she was sold again. One of her new owners was also her commander, Captain William Patterson of Edgecomb.

On this tragic voyage his younger brother, Corydon, served as first mate and his cousin, Charlie, as second. Also with him was his wife, Emma Smith Patterson, so gentle and so esteemed that people wondered why she had ever married him. For Captain Patterson was a hard man. This was not his first mutiny.

The ship sailed from New Orleans with a cargo of cotton-oil cake for England. As was often the case, Captain Patterson had had difficulty in getting a crew. Few local boys would sail with him, for he worked them too hard and fed them too little. Ready to sail, he had, aside from the mates, only a German steward named Aiken, a seaman named Wheeler, and a French cabin boy named Henry. Needing at least four more men, he managed to recruit three: George Miller, aged thirty-three, a Russian Finn; John Clew, twenty, an Englishman; and William Smith, twenty-three, an American. All were experienced sailors.

They sailed on March 5 by way of Boston. Almost as soon as they had started, Miller, a huge blond man who wore a high, yellow fur cap, began to make trouble. On March 12 Mrs. Patterson wrote in her diary: "We are blessed with good winds and weather, but disturbed by one bad sailor, a great powerful fellow who is very impudent." The next day he was put in irons. Captain Patterson's account follows: "We got the irons, but he refused to go into them, and we all three, the two mates and myself, tried to make him. He put his hand to his knife as if to draw it. I took hold of the blade, and, by giving it a quick twist, I broke it close to the handle. We overpowered him."

On March 15, Mrs. Patterson wrote again:

> This a.m. Miller asked Capt. what he could do to get out of irons and was answered "by doing his work like other men &c." Then the Capt. wrote a statement in the official log book for Miller to sign and one for the men to sign; then after getting their signatures he took M. out of irons. . . . We have heavy squalls which keeps me shaking.

The squalls continued, and the vessel, overloaded, sprang a leak so that the pumps had to be manned constantly. Though experienced on the sea, Mrs. Patterson was worried.

Mar. 21. It blew so heavy last night that at midnight we were obliged to "heave to" and all night and all day the vessel has been tumbling about and the cabins full of water; Will and all hands constantly drenched — Glass falling, rain ditto.

Mar. 23. The glass has speedily dropped all day and we have been fearing bad weather; to-night at eight o'clock it burst upon us in all its fury. O, such a fearful wind as is screaming and the seas are making wild havoc across the decks. Dashing and lashing everything in their terrible might.

The squalls soon turned into gales. The sea penetrated the water casks. Even with Miller out of chains, they were still short-handed. On March 25 Mrs. Patterson wrote:

O such a terrible day and evening in which my 33rd year of life is drawing to a close — a very heavy gale of wind is beating upon us, with such a fearful sea. To keep myself occupied I have been bailing water out of the cabin, for somehow, though the doors are closed, it gets in as fast as I can get it out.

For four days there was a lull. Then the winds began again.

Apr. 1, 1875. Such a terrible gale and such mountainous seas. Hove to at eight a.m. and at about noon how the wind did scream. I got up for a time to try to get the water out of the after cabin. Seas constantly coming over the quarter and two coming and lifting the sky-light and flooding cabins and state-rooms. Glass starting up a bit at night and little more moderate at midnight.

Apr. 2. But on this morning tending downward again and this p. m. heavy squalls of rain and wind. A heavy sea came over forward this p. m. and broke

in the galley doors and washed the boat from its lash-
ings.

Again the winds moderated. But there was other
trouble. On April 6, Mrs. Patterson wrote: "Things are not
moving pleasantly on board. The steward and the men are
pouty and only do what they are obliged to."

Their frame of mind was understandable. They had
been on deck continuously, drenched through, pumping,
and working the heavy sails. Their meals had been cold
and irregular. Water was rationed. Moreover, they had,
although Mrs. Patterson never acknowledged it, a tyranni-
cal captain to reckon with.

Then the gales returned and continued for ten days.
Mrs. Patterson describes those days:

Apr. 7. All day the glass has been falling till now
at seven p.m. it stands to nearly 29 7/10. We have a fresh
S.W. wind and O my heart fails me to bear what I fear
is coming. O, Father give me submission to Thy will
whatever it may be. 9 p.m. the glass a little lower;
weather looks more threatening.

Apr. 8. O, such a fearful night as was last night,
the glass was hardly up to 29 7/10. At half past ten we
had a squall and the wind changed into the N. Hove to
and reefed the spanker, and tried to reef the mainsail
but owing to such a body of water on deck found it
impossible. The vessel rolled most fearfully, washing
the men about decks. The mainsail is double reefed. The
wind is increasing, glass falling. O, Father still be our
support.

Apr. 10. Such a terrible gale as we are in. The glass
at 8 a.m. stood at 28 9/10. At noon the wind came from
the N.W. and I think I never heard it blow harder but
once in my life. A terrible sea came over aft, tearing
away the boards that had been nailed over the windows
& breaking in the windows, deluging cabins and

staterooms. I had been in bed but the terrific state of things called me up. I was up all last night as were all hands.

Apr. 11. The gale moderated before morning and at 5 a.m. ½ tenth above 30 but the weather looks threatening and another gale will soon be upon us. Been running the ship since 8 this morning under short sail. All are getting exhausted from so much hard work, wet and exposure, and God knows what the end will be. Lat. 36.47. Long. 43.28.

Apr. 12. The glass dropped a little last night but has stood on 30 today. Somewhat squally last night and we tore the foresail badly again. The sea still continued high and the weather does not look settled. We have made very slow progress thus far and I think we all feel disheartened. The decks are constantly flooded and the cabins very wet.

Apr. 13. This morning at about 6 the main boom broke in two. The wind was blowing fresh, but they managed to take care of it without injury to crew or vessel. Thank God. The glass has been falling but now at 8 p.m. starts up a bit. The wind is blowing a strong gale but we are running before it under reefed sails. Lat. 37.58. Long. 38.16.

Apr. 14. Was able to keep the vessel running all last night and today it has moderated but there is a very high sea and the vessel is rolling badly. Glass stands at 30. I am thankful that we got no gale last night or no worse one, for I much feared another terrible blow. 1800 more miles to the straits of Dover.

Apr. 15. All day has the glass been falling and now at 2 p.m. it is about 29 ⁶/₁₀ still with a downwind tendency. A fresh W. gale is blowing but we are still running under close sail. We have had some rain. Corry is nearly sick from incessant toil and exposure, and O, what is to become of us, God alone knows.

Apr. 16. Lat. 39.42. Long. 33. 5 weeks since we left the bar. Hove to at 10 last night and have been running since 8 this a.m. but there is a fearful sea running and great quantities of water come on board. I can't tell when we have had a smooth sea, or dry cabins or deck. O, that the Lord would be pleased to send us fine weather. This is a terrible passage.

On April 17 the weather changed into calm. Mrs. Patterson felt a great relief.

Apr. 18. Bless God for this fine day. A nice fair breeze and the smoothest sea we have seen in a long time; still the vessel being deep the water keeps the deck wet. I read one of Spurgeon's sermons today and have commenced reading Father Taylor's Life.

Apr. 19. Lat. 42.26. Long. 26.54. Such a lovely day with a fair wind and dry decks. I have been on the main deck today; I am sure I cannot tell when I was there before. Two vessels in sight today. We shall be 60 days making the passage but if we can get there in that time, all in safely, I know I shall be thankful.

But the calm only preceded disaster. For more than a month the crew had battled almost continuous high winds and heavy seas. There was still no rest. The foresail had to be taken down, mended, and put up again. The boom had to be spliced. The vessel was still leaking. Food was short and water brackish. On the night of April 20, mutiny broke out.

Captain Patterson's own account, written in the ship's log, begins thus:

At 11:45 midnight was called by George Miller who said in an excited tone and manner that John had broken his leg and was dangerously hurt and wished me to come forward at once to help the man. I at once went out of my room and George went on deck but I saw by

196

his movements all was not right. So I went out to find the mates and see what watch it was. Saw by the clock that it was the 2nd mate's watch, it being then 11:50. Then I went aft to the wheel and could not find him — then went to the mate's room and found that he was not in his room then went on deck and called for him but got no reply from anyone. This I thought very strange as the night was fine and I could be heard all over the decks while I was calling the mates. George came again and very excitedly asked why I didn't go forward to assist the man as he feared he would die if not attended.

Though the log does not record it, it was Mrs. Patterson who sensed what was happening and dissuaded him from going, thus saving his life. His report continues:

I then went into the cabin to arm myself as I could hear nothing from the mates and didn't believe what George was telling me as he seemed wild and excited and was so anxious to get me forward. When he found I would not go but came into the cabin, he left and went forward. During this time I saw he held his right hand behind him and he seemed to be holding something in his hand which made me more suspicious of him. I then called the steward who I found already up in his room. He came out at once and I sent him to see if he could find the mates, but he could not hear anything from [them] and feared that they were murdered. The steward said that the men were all standing forward talking together. I also went aft and asked the man at the wheel where the mates were. He said that the 2nd mate had gone forward to reef the outer jib a short time before and that the mate had left the quarter about 10 minutes before since which he had seen nothing of them. He said he saw two men on the jib boom and men moving around decks. He also heard someone cry out Oh Oh as if hurt but heard nothing more.

Thus Captain Patterson recorded his brother's death.

Though his words were matter-of-fact, he felt it deeply. Corydon was his only brother. His mother had entrusted him to his care. Charlie was his favorite cousin. Both boys were young, Corydon, twenty-six, Charlie, thirty-three. Both were sons of widowed mothers. His account continues:

> The steward and I again went forward hoping to get some tidings of the mates. . . . The crew were seen forward saying that they would not hurt him if he would come. We asked where the mates were but got no reply. I told the man at the wheel not to leave the wheel or attempt to go forward; if he did I would shoot him down. Could get nothing from him as to the works of the crew or what they intended to do. He said he feared the mates were overboard. All night the vessel was under full sail, and I feared a gale as the glass was falling but had no means of getting sail off the vessel or keeping the vessel pumped out. I kept a sharp watch over the men all night, hoping they had the mates secured and confined in some place forward and at daylight we could effect their release. . . . At about 6 a.m. heard a knocking at the cabin entrance to the lazarette — asked who was there and recognized Henry's (cabin boy) voice saying for me to let him into the cabin. He said he had been gagged, bound and put into the forehold and secured there; that he had got clear and come aft over the cargo to inform us but knew nothing of the fate of the mates.

At daylight Captain Patterson found the men forward of the forecastle with all kinds of missiles — bottles, broken grindstone, clubs, and capstan bars. He tried to question them, but they remained silent and surly. He sounded the pumps and found to his relief that the vessel had not been injured. He then called on the men to submit to his authority. Their reply was a shower of weapons. Captain Patterson fired his revolver, and they fled for shelter into the deck house — not more than ten feet square.

Then the captain and steward prepared for the attacks which they realized would be forthcoming. All firearms — three revolvers and a double-barreled gun — were got in readiness. At five o'clock in the morning, finding that all the mutineers wer dozing, the captain hit upon the idea of nailing up the door of the deck house.

This done, he again called upon the men to surrender. Again they refused. After removing the funnel from the smoke hole, he poured bucket after bucket of boiling water upon them. They still were adamant. Then he fired his revolver through the window and kept firing until all the men were wounded. Miller had seven wounds, five in the leg; John Clew had two severe ones beneath his left ribs; Smith had been shot through wrist, shoulders, and fingers. Still it was thirty-six hours before they surrendered and confessed. Captain Patterson's log follows:

> George Miller admitted killing the mate and that Wm Smith and John Clew helped to throw him overboard and Wm Smith admitted that he threw the 2nd mate overboard from the bowsprit. We then heavily ironed and secured the men and dressed their wounds. During the p.m. got sail off the vessel and secured the foresail and jibs as best we could. Found the boat cast adrift and expect the men attempted to escape from the vessel in her, but the wind blowing strong and the vessel moving so fast they could not succeed.

All this time the wind had blown. Now it blew stronger. On the night of the mutiny the foretop sail had been torn to pieces and the foresail blown from the mast. There had been twenty-two inches of water in the hold. Now the water deepened. Miller and Smith, both seriously injured, were chained to the pump and forced to work it.

John Clew, so they thought, was dying. They had little confidence in the loyalty of the other men, especially of Jake, the helmsman. Their only hope lay in sighting a ship that would give them help. But no ship appeared. Mrs. Patterson's diary reveals her distress:

> 22nd April, 1875. O, must I, can I write the terrible truth that Corry and Charles have been thrown overboard by those fiends. They acknowledge having done it because they were tired of the vessel, they say, & wanted to get clear of her. O, we are overwhelmed with grief and know not how to bear it.

> 23rd. O, the weary, torturing hours of the days and nights. Are these terrible things true or are we dreaming. Corry, Charles, O, where are your billow-tossed bodies tonight?

What Mrs. Patterson's diary does not reveal is her courage. Having by her judgment saved her husband's life, she continued to protect it. Hour after hour she stood watch so that he might sleep a little. She moved fearlessly among the men, talking to George Miller, and reading the Bible to Clew. On April 25 she wrote:

> A South West gale beating upon us. I managed in the p.m. to get out to the forecastle to see John once more. Have tried to point him to the Saviour. He will soon die.

With concern not only for his soul, but for her husband's reputation, she induced this confession:

> I John Clew, beliving that I am about to die, do solemnly make this statement: on Tuesday night of April 20th between the hours of ten and eleven, I should judge, I was, while sleeping in my berth, called to the door of the forecastle by Wm Smith. Reaching the door, he, Smith, told me that he and George Miller were that night going to kill and throw overboard the Capt. and

officers of the vessel and that I must help do the work.
I replied, "I cannot, it is not in my power." He (Smith)
then said to me, "If you don't help us we will serve you
the same as the rest." I then answered, "Well, I suppose
I shall have to then." Smith said he had already thrown
the 2d Mate overboard. This was the first information I
had of any such intended crime, but Smith told me at
this time that he had been planning to do it all the
passage because he had been kept up in his watches
below and had so much work to do. Geo. Miller was up
when I was called, but I don't know how long he had
been up. Smith then left and he and Miller went aft,
threw the Mate overboard and then called the Capt.
When the Capt. came out I stood abaft the forward house
armed with a capstan bar, having told them I would not
go any farther aft. I do not know what they intended to
do with the Capt's wife, neither do I know what they
intended to do with the Steward, boy Henry, the seaman
Bake or the vessel — I cannot tell why I did not go aft
and inform the Capt. of this meeting as I had before
promised to do, and I now deeply regret that I did not
do so—

I had never had any talk with Miller about this as
he and I have not spoken to each other since we had a
row about who should sweep the forecastle—

I have never been ill-treated on board this vessel,
neither to my knowledge has anyone else been.

his
John X Clew
mark

On April 26 they saw a sail. "Toward night we saw
a barque standing to the southward," Mrs. Patterson
wrote, "but could not reach her to signal. This is the first
vessel we have seen save one in the night. Send us help,
O Father."

But when no help came, Capt. Patterson broke
down. For six days he had recorded factually in ink the

201

location of the ship, the weather, the behavior of the mutineers, even the deaths of his brother and cousin. On this day he wrote almost illegibly in pencil. "26th April 6 a.m. We don't know in whose hands we are things look *dark Black* who are friends and who are foes I fear all but one and my wife — Lord deliver her and me no sail in sight — may one soon appear so we can get help — mates murdered and thrown overboard we may follow them — my *dear dear* Brother is gone."

The next morning they saw another sail — this one to the northward — and for a little while there was hope. But the sail disappeared. That night at dusk they saw another. All night they waited fearfully. In the morning the vessel, a Norwegian bark, got their signal, and her captain gave them one of his sailors. With the extra hand, they managed, but the strain had told. On April 28 Mrs. Patterson wrote: "It seems as tho' I can see the flesh leaving Will day by day." And again on May 1: "Will and I are about worn out with constant watching and suffering. While one sleeps the other works."

On May 2, approaching land, they knew they were safe. But they felt little satisfaction. In London all was confusion. Hardly had the American consul taken the mutineers into custody than the story spread, and the ship was swarming with the sympathetic and the curious. Reporters came aboard, asking questions. Again and again Captain and Mrs. Patterson had to go back over the terrible happenings. Letters were brought on board, among them letters for Corydon and Charlie. Word had to be sent home.

The strain showed on Mrs. Patterson so badly that her husband urged her to leave the ship. On May 8 she wrote: "I left the ship for the first time this eve and took a drive but I had no enjoyment & was soon tired. Everyone is so kind but O the heartache in Edgecomb today. I can only think of those two aged widowed mothers and their loving hearts bleeding & broken. O you *dear* mothers, would God I had died for *them*, & you had your two boys — O my Father, comfort & sustain those dear hearts."

The crowds kept coming. The hearing was ahead, and Mrs. Patterson must have been uneasy about it. On May 10 she was persuaded to visit an acquaintance twenty miles from London. Though she had planned to stay away three days, she stayed less than two. Back on the ship she could neither eat nor sleep. "O, my heart and brain," she wrote, "how much longer can I keep up?" Once she started for a church service, but was too tired to go on. Once Captain Patterson took her for a drive. "Went to Hyde Park," she wrote, "and visited Madam Tussard's bazaar. Her wax figures are really wonderful, but should we say we enjoyed the day we should speak falsely. When I see anything I could enjoy the thoughts shut it out. O Corry, O Charlie, you dear kind hearted boys." A month after their deaths, she expressed concern for her sanity: "I hope my mind will not leave me so entirely as to unfit me for the remaining days of life."

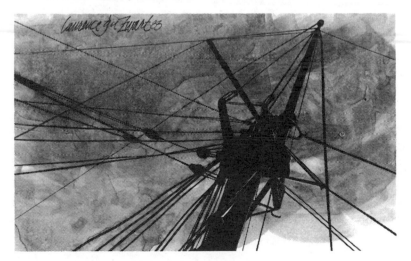

On May 26 William Smith was removed from the hospital to a prison, where he made a statement "full of falsehoods," Mrs. Patterson wrote, adding, "Should not suppose anything ought to shock me now." Her concern for the hearing and its effect on her husband took the edge off her grief. She began to insist that he leave the ship whenever he could. On June 8 they went to Windsor. A few days later she had her picture taken to please him.

On June 7 the three mutineers came up in the Bow Street police court. "Such a statement as Miller made," Mrs. Patterson wrote. "Clew said but little and Smith gave his same story. They are remanded to the U. S. for trial for murder." Exactly what was said cannot be told, for the records are not available. The newspapers, however, brought out the fact, censoriously, that Miller, though grievously wounded, had been chained three days to the pump and forced to work it. But generally sympathy was still with the Pattersons.

On June 17 they sailed for home. As Mrs. Patterson's anxiety concerning the hearing eased, her grief returned.

> June 18. Pilot left this morning & and we have been sailing and anchoring as tides and winds favor. Will we ever reach home! O, how dim and misty all the future looks. I have so longed for a home of my own but now I seem to *long* for nothing — I only float.

On Sept. 22 the mutineers were tried and on October 14, sentenced to be hanged. But meantime sentiment was changing. Certain influential people became interested in the case, and numerous petitions were sent to President Grant, asking commutation of their sentence to life imprisonment. One petition was signed by the Governor of Maine, the Ex-Governor, and the Governor-Elect. It read in part:

> The convicts are natives of this State and well

204

known to many of our citizens, who have informed us that they were young men of excellent character, and that if they had been allowed to testify in their own behalf (as is permitted by the laws of this state), there would have appeared reason for doubt as to whether the killing was not in self-defense.

Another, signed by the Governor of Massachusetts and the Mayor of Boston read:

> We are also informed, and believe, that the voyage had been a very long and stormy one, that the vessel was short-handed, and the crew had been for a large part of the voyage kept almost incessantly on deck, and had been overworked and insufficiently supplied with proper food, and had been subjected to such prolonged and cruel treatment by the Captain and the Mates as to drive them to desperation, and that the crime was committed suddenly and under circumstances of great provocation. We are persuaded that if the crew had not been treated with prolonged and extraordinary cruelty, the crime would never have been committed, and that it was committed on a sudden impulse by men disheartened and desperate from long continued overwork, ill-treatment and hard usage.

Another petition of essentially the same nature was signed by two bishops of the Methodist Episcopal Church, four presiding elders, the dean of Boston University, and sixty-eight other ministers of the Gospel. Later there were also petitions of the Knights of Labor and the Sailors' and Firemen's Union of New York.

Captain Patterson had some sympathizers, most of them gained by the activity of his wife, who with tireless persistence sought support for him. (Among his papers are many penciled defenses, obviously first-draft letters sent to public officials — one of them to the President, protesting any clemency for the men. There were also letters to editors who, in their papers, had sided with the condemned.) But gradually, due, not doubt, to a growing number of stories told to reporters by men who had once sailed with Captain Patterson and vowed never to sail with him again, public sentiment began to swing in the direction of the mutineers. The earlier sentence was retracted. John Clew was acquitted of murder and sent to Charlestown prison for ten years, charged only with mutiny. George Miller and William Smith were sentenced to life imprisonment at Thomaston for the crime of piracy. Miller died there in 1894. Smith was pardoned in 1903, a year after Mrs. Patterson's death, which was unquestionably hastened by this experience.

She never got over it. On April 20, 1883, she added this note to the last page of her diary, begun on the *Jefferson Borden*.

> April 20, 1883. Eight years since that terrible tragedy occurred. No one on earth save Will & myself can begin to realize the horror, the dreadful wretchedness & agony of the time — & it clings to us, & shivers the marrow of our bones & almost palsies our heart at every thought of it. O, we trust God has in tender care those poor innocent helpless boys.

Her husband, who never made another major voyage, became morose after his wife's death and was committed for a time to a state mental hospital. He was eventually released and died alone in a Wiscasset hotel in 1922.

The fate of the *Jefferson Borden* was tragic to the end. After the mutiny, she was put up for sale. Finding no buyers, the owners changed her name to *Arcana*. Five years later during a terrific storm she went down just off a lighthouse in the Bay of Fundy, with all on board.

Village School

he old Edgecomb schoolhouse still stands at the turn of the road that leads to Boothbay Harbor. It was like most other schoolhouses of its era, with a single door, opening into an entry used for wood and wraps. It had one main room, with a center aisle, on either side of which stood rows of double desks, fronted by recitation benches. It had the usual stove with its long rusty pipe. It had a badly lighted blackboard. It had a water pail with a common dipper.

But in one sense it was unique. Probably few schoolhouses have ever been more drafty. On the top of a hill, completely unprotected, it caught the full force of the wind and trembled, sometimes staggered, under it. When the wind came from the north, it roared in the eaves and rattled the doors. It slapped the rope on the flagpole. It quickened the fire and sent puffs of smoke down the chimney. It drove in the snow and rain, making little drifts or pools along the window sills. It rattled the maps, blew the dipper from its hook, and set the pointer swaying.

During the last of the eighteenth and the entire

207

nineteenth centuries, all village children attended this school. They studied the same subjects. They used, quite literally, the same books. They turned down the same pages. On the same flyleaves they wrote comparable comments:

> When this you spy
> Remember I.

> All I want is a little spot
> On which to write forget me not . . .

They carried the same kind of food in their dinner pails — stripped fish, hard-boiled eggs, doughnuts, cold biscuit, and cold coffee, sometimes in a patent-medicine bottle.

Their teacher was hardly more advanced than they were. Sometimes he had been graduated from the academy in Wiscasset; sometimes he had completed only the same eight grades he was teaching. He was paid three dollars a week — later raised to four dollars — and if he came "from away" he was boarded round among the parents of his scholars. A strong arm was an essential to him, for he had the fires to tend, the floors to sweep, and the cane to wield when it was necessary.

Under his direction the young scholars followed a course of study laid out by the school board. They had no watered-down curriculum, as their textbooks will testify. They studied common fractions, decimal fractions, percentage, equation of payments, insurance, custom-house business, coins and currencies, not only those of European countries but those of Asia as well.

They studied exchange, memorizing long tables from which such problems as this one could, supposedly, be solved:

> A merchant in London remits to Amsterdam £1000
> at the rate of 18d. per guilder, directing his correspon-

dent at Amsterdam to remit the same to Paris at 2 francs 10 centimes per guilder, less ½ percent for his commission; but the exchange between Amsterdam and Paris happened to be, at the time the order was received, at 2 francs 20 centimes per guilder. The merchant at London, not apprised of this, drew upon Paris at 25 francs per pound sterling. Did he gain or lose, and how much per cent? Ans. Gain, 16 ⁵⁶/₇₅ percent.

They studied what was called alligation and attacked such problems as this:

A merchant has spices, some at 18c a pound, some at 24c, some at 48c, and some at 60c. How much of each sort must be taken that the mixture must be worth 40c a pound? Ans. 1 lb. at 18c; 1 lb. at 24c; 1 lb. at 48c; 1½ lbs. at 60c.

They studied involution, finding, for instance, the value of .045 raised to the fourth power. They studied evolution, considering both rational and surd roots. They studied arithmetic progression:

A certain school consists of 19 teachers and scholars, whose ages form an arithmetical series, the youngest is 3 years old, the oldest 39. What is the common difference in their ages? Ans. 2 years.

Then they tackled problems in geometrical progression:

If I were to buy 30 oxen, giving 2c for the first ox, 4c for the second, 8c for the third, etc., what would be the price of the last ox? Ans. $10,737, 418.24.

They studied annuities:

A father presents to his daughter, for 8 years, a rental of $70 per annum, payable yearly, and its reversion for the 12 years succeeding to his son. What is the percent value of the gift to his son, allowing 4 percent compound interest? Ans. $480.03.

Finally they studied mensuration:

What is the government tonnage of Noah's Ark, admitting its length to have been 479 feet, its breadth 80 feet, and its depth 48 feet. Ans. 15,517 $\frac{17}{19}$ tons.

It is astonishing that they had either the time or the heart to write with levity in the margins!

In grammar, their text divided neatly into orthography, etymology, syntax, and prosody. (The print of their text was so fine that one wonders how, on a dark day, they could read it at all.) First they studied the parts of speech. They classified nouns, compared adjectives, and conjugated verbs.

> If I be loved
> If he be loved
> If thou be loved

Then they began parsing, following this perhaps significant model: "The patient ox submits to the yoke, and meekly performs the labor of him. Submits is a verb, because it signifies action. Ox is a noun, because it is the name of a thing."

Following parsing, they began analysis of such admonitory sentences as: "Children who disobey their parents deserve punishment. The subject of the principal clause is children; the predicate is deserve, and the object is punishment. . . . "

Passing through punctuation, they took up the figures of rhetoric, and later turned to scanning poetry.

Most of the scholars seem to have taken grammar rather lightly, for the exercises provoked repeated marginal response. After "She reads well and writes neatly," someone has written, "You don't say"; after "Whither shall I go?" — "to grass"; after "This came in fashion when I was young" — "and frisky"; after "There is not the least hope for her recovery" — "too bad."

They studied geography, history and physiology, learning the names of every muscle and bone. In the 1880s a new subject was added — elocution. The text was called the *Elocutionary Reader*. According to its plan, the scholars first applied themselves to definitions. They learned about tonics, subtonics, triphthongs, labials:

> In sounding the tones, the organs should be fully opened, and the stream of sound from the throat should be thrown, as much as possible, directly upward against the roof of the mouth. These elements should open with an abrupt and explosive force, and then diminish gradually and equably to the end.

Next they studied expression, with its general divisions of emphasis, slur, inflection, modulation, monotone, personation. Words and phrases to be slurred were italicized:

> "But now," *whispered the dear girl*, "it is evening; the sun, *that rejoices*, has finished his daily toil; man, *that labors*, has finished his; I, *that suffer*, have finished mine." Just then, her dull ear caught a sound. It was the sound, *though muffled and deadened like the ear that heard it*, of horsemen advancing.

Next they approached inflection and modulation. Here again they were given specific instructions: High pitch must be used when calling from a distance. (Probably

no trouble here, since every scholar had his cows to call.)
Moderate pitch must be used for conversation, description,
and calm reasoning; low pitch for reverence, awe, sublimity
and tender emotions.

Monotone, they learned, was to be used only for the
ghostly and the supernatural. (This must have been quickly
passed over. Too many used it anyway, and for neither of
these reasons.) Next came personation. This was livelier,
since, after some training, it permitted double participa-
tion. Sometimes an exercise called for a boy and girl to
perform together, no doubt eliciting excitement and a
general titter.

> *He:* Dost thou love wandering?
> Whither wouldst thou go?
> Dream'st thou, sweet daughter,
> of a land more fair? Dost thou
> not love these aye-blue streams
> that flow? These spicy forests?
> and this golden air?
> *She:* Oh, yes, I love the woods and
> streams, so gay,
> And more than all, O Father, I
> love thee;
> Yet would I fain be wandering —
> far away,
> Where such things never were, nor
> e'er shall be.
> *He:* Speak, mine own daughter with the
> sun-bright locks!
> To what pale, banished region
> wouldst thou roam?
> *She:* O, Father, let us find our frozen
> rocks.
> Let's seek that country of all
> countries — Home!

Once the rules and exercises were mastered, the scholars were ready to try their wings. But not — let it be quickly said — without guidance. One can imagine the room quiet, a scholar by his desk, his tongue carefully placed, his breath drawn properly, waiting for a tap on the call bell to begin his recitation.

Not only was the speaking voice trained. So also was laughter, "its 32 well-defined varieties" being described as an art. The elocution class could have had little use for laughter, for in the entire textbook there was not a single selection that might provoke it. There were sighs for home and loved ones; there were deathbed scenes, funeral trains, interments. There were tales of parting and renunciation; there were tears beyond count. But for laughter, art or no, the textbook offered no opportunity.

As the lessons progressed, gestures, of course, were added. For orations, the clenched fist and shaken forefinger did well enough, but poetry demanded gestures that were subtle and refined:

> I saw the blue Rhine sweep along
> *(palm shading eyes).*
> I heard or seemed to hear
> *(hand cupped to ear).*
> The German songs we used to sing, in chorus
> sweet and clear;
> And down the pleasant river
> *(dropping movement of left arm)*
> and up the slanting hill
> *(right arm sharply raised).*
> The echoing chorus sounded through the evening
> calm and still.
> *(Hand to ear again).*

One wishes one might have heard them on some windy day when the pitch would have of necessity been high, whatever the emotion. One wishes, too, that, especially on some dark Monday in March, when the mud had reached the boot-tops, he might have listened in on those thirty-two different varieties of laughter!

Village Library

n 1821, leaders in Edgecomb started to talk about a library. It was not the first time the subject had come up. In 1806 one group had gone so far as to submit a petition in town meeting where it was roundly rejected. But fifteen years had brought changes. Well-rooted now, the village had begun to flower. Literacy was common and so was travel. Hardly a week passed that some ship did not return to the Sheepscot from ports of Asia and Europe. Coastwise schooners took passengers to Boston, where they visited public buildings and returned, their horizons widened, to tell of the sights they had seen. Maine was no longer a District, but a State, and its people felt a new pride. This time, without asking the town for support, some of the citizens decided that they themselves would start and run the library.

It was an earnest group, opening its first meeting with a prayer. Then working together, one member suggesting a word, another a phrase, it drew up a constitution. Officers were elected and a campaign for members

215

begun. Some, eager for books — and perhaps for sociability — joined promptly. Some, interested, but weighing, no doubt, the annual dues of fifty cents (an amount not to be taken lightly) delayed. Others, suspicious of novels, held out until they knew what books might be offered.

The library opened with forty books, most of which must have been donated by the members themselves. There were histories: *History of New England, History of the Inquisition, Ecclesiastical History of Maine, History of England, History of Greece, History of the United States, History of Martyrs, Ancient History, Manners and Customs of Nations.* There were biographies of Washington, Putnam, Franklin, Martin Luther, William Tell, Thomas Spencer, Stephen Decatur, Lafayette and, oddly, Mohammed. (One was entitled *Sacred Female Biographies*.) There were travel books: *Journal of a Tour, Voyages, Travels in South Africa.*

But most of the books concerned moral teaching. Among them were these: *Self-Knowledge, The Force of Truth, Christian Philosophy, Management of the Tongue, Christian Principles of Politeness, Evidences of the Christian Religion, and Universal Preceptor.*

As the years passed, more books were added. In 1829 there were seventy, all of the same general sort. Those who worried about novels must have given up their apprehensions, for unless it was *Memoirs of Miss Smith* or *Solitude Sweetened* no worldy book was among them.

But gradually a few such books crept in. Two of them remain. Both are books of etiquette. Both are badly worn. (By feminine hands, one fancies.) One is the *Habits of Good Society*, the other is *Decorum*. They must have been late additions, for they were published after 1850. The vicarious satisfaction they brought can only be imagined.

To one accustomed to a morning splash at the pump, and, at best, a weekly scrub in the wash tub, how fascinating to learn the rule for the bath:

216

The first thing to be attended to after rising is the BATH. We must not suppose because a limb looks clean that it does not need washing. However white the skin may appear, we should use the bath once a day, and in summer, if convenient, twice. . . .

To one used to taking what came out of the teakettle, how interesting this:

The most cleansing bath is a warm one from 96° to 100°, into which the whole body is immersed. . . . The cold bath of from 60° to 70°, on the other hand, cleanses less, but invigorates more. It should therefore be avoided by persons of full temperament. A tepid bath, varying from 85° to 95° is, perhaps, the safest of all.

How illuminating, too, the rules of procedure:

Take a sponge nearly a foot in length and six inches broad and fill it completely with water. The part of the body which should first be attacked is the stomach. It is there that the most heat has collected during the night, and the application of cold water quickens the circulation at once, and sends the blood which has been employed in digestion round the whole body. The head should next be soused, unless the person be of full habit when the head should be attacked before the feet touch the cold water at all.

How those who habitually got up at four or, at the latest five, must have sighed over this:

No person in good health should remain in bed after seven o'clock, or half-past seven in spring and summer. She may then be down stairs at eight, and without taking a long and fatiguing walk, saunter in the garden a little.

One wonders how many times these passages must have been read aloud in the presence of sons and husbands:

It is painful to see the amount of ease with which some men sit on the edge of a chair, but at the same time the manner in which others throw themselves back and stretch forward their legs savours too much of familiarity. You may cross your legs if you like, but not hug your knees or your toes. Straddling a chair and tilting it up may be pardonable in a bachelor's room, but not in a lady's drawing room.

One must never smoke, nor even ask to smoke, in the company of the fair. One must never smoke, again, in the streets; that is, in daylight. One must never smoke in a room inhabited at times by the ladies. Thus, a well-bred man who has a wife or sister will not offer to smoke in the dining room after dinner. One must never smoke in a public place, where ladies are or might be, for instance, a flower show or promenade. One must never smoke, without consent, in the presence of a clergyman. But if you smoke, and if you are in the company of smokers, and are to wear your clothes in the presence of ladies afterwards, you must change them to smoke in.

Decorum, completely dilapidated, contains largely model letters; letters of invitation, formal and informal; letters of introduction; letters of congratulation and condolence; letters proposing, accepting, and declining marriage. It is doubtful if any Edgecomb girl ever received such a letter as this, but how thrilling it must have been to study it.

> Dear Miss _____:
>
> I am conscious that it may be presumptuous for me to address this note; yet feel that an honorable declaration of my feeling toward you is due to my own heart and my future happiness. I first met you to admire; your beauty and intelligence served to increase that admiration to a feeling of personal interest; and now, I am free to confess, your virtues and graces have inspired in me a sentiment of love — not the sentiment which finds its gratification in the civilities of friendly intercourse, but which asks in return a heart and a hand for life.
>
> This confession I make freely and openly to you, feeling that you will give it all the consideration it deserves. If I am not deceived, it cannot cause you pain; but, if any circumstance has weighed with you — any interest in another person, or any family obstacle, forbid you to encourage my suit, then I leave it to your candor to make such a reply to this note as seems proper. I shall wait your answer with some anxiety, and therefore hope you may reply at your earliest convenience.
>
> Believe me, dear lady, with feelings of true regard,
>
> Yours, most sincerely,

How many girls, for the excitement of it, made a copy of this model (filling in the blanks perhaps) just to see how it would look.

> Dear Mr._____:
>
> Your note of the . . . reached me duly. Its tone

of candor requires from me what it would be improper to refuse — an equally candid answer.

I sincerely admire you. Your qualities of heart and mind have impressed me favorably, and, now that you tell me I have won your love, I am conscious that I too am regarding you more highly and tenderly than comports with a mere friend's relation.

Do not, however, give this confession too much weight, for, after all, we may both be deceived in regard to the nature of our esteem, and I should, therefore, suggest, for the present, the propriety of your calling upon me at my father's house on occasional evenings; and will let time and circumstances determine if it is best for us to assume more serious relation to one another than have heretofore existed.

I am, sir, with true esteem,

Yours, sincerely,

But such books were the exception. In 1860 the library boasted 157 volumes. Its range had widened. Shakespeare was there; so were the essays of Francis Bacon. Poetry had found its way to the shelves with Milton and Wordsworth. There were even a few scientific books, among them a textbook on chemistry and a treatise on the stars. Still the books of moral value predominated. To them a new kind had been added — books on temperance. (These held arguments against the use of alcohol, statistics of its evils, pleas for prohibition, sentimental tales of drunkards and the misery they brought.) By 1880 the total number of books had reached 300.

The cultural high point of the year was the annual meeting, held at four o'clock on Christmas day. Earlier, perhaps at two, a committee gathered to inspect the books. One thinks of them around a table, a lamp burning if the day was dark, turning pages, looking for dogears or pencil marks, sniffing disapprovingly as they caught the smell of fish or tobacco, frowning at a spot of kerosene or molasses, and speculating on the culprit. One thinks of them checking bindings or pasting pages, dipping in here or there as they worked, or perhaps exchanging recommendations. One sees them studying the cards on the covers to find out who had taken out *Management of the Tongue* or to learn what the minister had been reading.

Just before four o'clock they drew up their report. (In 1825 it was this: "The books were in tolerable condition with few exceptions.") At four-thirty came the annual address, given by some distinguished member of the society. One such address remains. It was delivered in 1823 by Rufus Sewall, son of an early minister of the town, who had been entirely self-taught. It began thus:

> Man is a social being. Example and advice have a surprising influence upon him. His happiness, his success in whatever he attempts, his character and his improvement in knowledge and virtue, or his degradation in vice and misery depend in a great measure upon the character of those with whom he associates and the connections he forms in society.
>
> Do any wish to know the history of their own country, the causes which led our venerable ancestors to assert its independence, the means by which it was achieved and the character of the patriots who spilt their blood and hazarded their lives and fortunes in its defense? By reading they may obtain this knowledge and find every circumstance relating to it clearly and distinctly traced.
>
> Are any desirous of becoming acquainted with the history of other countries and nations? In this way they may satisfy themselves. Are any anxious to know the manners and customs of nations? In this way they

may follow the intrepid and inquisitive traveler and visit all the known nations from the northern to the southern pole and from the rising to the setting sun. . . . Are any disposed to know what have been the effects of unrestrained passions and lusts which have been the fruitful source of wars and fighting among mankind? Let them inquire of the faithful historian and he will inform them that a trifling dispute has arisen between two powerful nations, that ambition, obstinacy and selfishness prevented its settlement. . . .

Are any inquiring what is the moral state of the world? By reading they may satisfy all their inquiries. They may follow the devoted missionary in his researches in heathen lands and behold myriads of the human race devoted to idolatry and ignorance and superstition. . . .

These words were from a man whose father had been, until manhood, illiterate. They were addressed to men and women in a place where, less than two hundred years before, men would have "cut one another's throats for beaver."

Are any desirous of becoming acquainted with the history of other countries and nations? In this way they may satisfy themselves. Are any anxious to know the manners and customs of nations? In this way they may follow the intrepid and inquisitive traveler and visit all the known nations from the northern to the southern pole and from the rising to the setting sun. . . . Are any disposed to know what have been the effects of unrestrained passions and lusts which have been the fruitful source of wars and fighting among mankind? Let them inquire of the faithful historian and he will inform them that a trifling dispute has arisen between two powerful nations, that ambition, obstinacy and selfishness prevented its settlement. . . .

222

Are any inquiring what is the moral state of the world? By reading they may satisfy all their inquiries. They may follow the devoted missionary in his researches in heathen lands and behold myriads of the human race devoted to idolatry and ignorance and superstition. . . .

These words were from a man whose father had been, until manhood, illiterate. They were addressed to men and women in a place where, less than two hundred years before, men would have "cut one another's throats for beaver."

Village Postmaster

he Edgecomb store was on the county road, now Route 27, beside the village graveyard. It was a large, square-fronted building, painted dark yellow with a brown trim. Upstairs and in the back were living quarters, and along the front was a covered piazza.

Fessenden Stone owned it. He was a good-humored, easy-going man whom everybody liked. Much of his time was spent on the river or open sea in his dory taking in cod, mackerel and lobster, which he shipped to New York. Then the store was run by his wife, Fanny, the postmaster, who held that office for forty-seven years, the longest term of service of any postmaster in the United States.

It was a typical country store of the period. Just inside the door, on the right, was the hardware: screws, nails, bolts, padlocks, bits, hinges, hammers, axes, calking irons, rope, wire, cowbells, clothespins. Beyond were the yard goods: percale, ginghams, oil cloths, bolt piled on bolt, in a medley of colors. Beside them stood the thread cabinet, the spools arranged like rainbows.

Beyond the yard goods was the cheese case, fronted by kegs of salt mackerel, tongues and sounds, pickled tripe and dried slack-salted pollack. Next to them were the scales, and, conveniently to the right, the coffee grinder. On the shelf behind it were staples: soda, salt, spices, vanilla, tea. Beneath were barrels of beans, yellow-eyed, pea, and kidney. (The pork that would go with them was kept in the cellar, along with the vinegar and kerosene.)

In the corner, to the right, within easy reach, was the sugar barrel. Against the back wall were shelves holding overalls, oilskins, lumber jackets, heavy-weight underwear, socks, and corsets (the latter to be tried on with Fanny's help in the kitchen). Below was the barrel of Barbados molasses.

To the left was the post office, glass-fronted, with fifty or so numbered compartments and a window where you could ask for your mail. A letter slot was beneath it. On the far wall, perforated with tack holes, was a place for notices: things lost or found, hunting and fishing regulations, pictures and descriptions of criminals at large, posters of Ice Cream Socials and Grange suppers.

Behind the post office was a long candy counter, holding Boston Baked Beans, each one a succulent peanut covered with dark-red sugared candy, sold for a cent a pot; licorice Nigger Babies; Necco wafers in plain or assorted flavors; bouncing balls (tough globes of speckled gelatin that could be jerked on an elastic string); spongy marshmallows; peppermint sticks circled with rings for your finger; chocolate-drops shaped like beehives; sticks of horehound; candy hearts bearing tender sentiments that blurred at first sucking; barberpole gum.

On shelves above were the patent medicines: Dr.

Mattison's Indian Emmenagogue; Dr. Churchill's Hypophosphite of Lime and Soda; Ayer's Cherry Pectoral; Atwood's Bitters; Fletcher's Castoria; paregoric; sweet spirits of niter; golden oil; Colby's Liniment, patented by the farmer in charge of the poorhouse in Wiscasset; Lydia Pinkham's Vegetable Compound, to be asked for only of Fanny, with a significant nod in its direction and a look that solicited sympathy.

Then came the whip rack holding the Dictators, the Park Pride, and the Giant Crackers. Beyond that was the tobacco shelf where the Pippins and the plugs (Sickle and Climax) together with the cutters were kept. Here also was the snuff.

Hanging from the ceiling were strings of burnished alewives, dried apricots, catnip, and a single bunch of bananas. One of these once held a tarantula which, captured and placed in a jar, cried, people said, like a baby. In the back of the room, near the center, was the pot-bellied stove with a sawdust box beside it for the convenience of the loafers.

At holiday seasons other things were crowded in. For Fourth of July there were firecrackers, torpedoes, cap pistols, sometimes a few Roman candles; for Christmas there were blocks, dolls, dolls' heads for the thrifty, dolls' dishes. There were toys, knives, whistles, games (Flinch, Checkers, Tiddledewinks, Old Maid). There was ribbon candy. There were marbles, writing paper, colored pencils. . . .

Everywhere there was a smell, an exciting blend of dry fish and new leather; of molasses and oil cloth; of fresh ground coffee and cider vinegar; of kerosene and Lenox soap. It was probably the cleanest store in the State of Maine, even as it is today.

There are very few pictures of postmaster Fanny

Stone, for she had no vanity and seldom stopped long enough to have a picture taken. She was tall and thin — the build that is known as wiry — with abundant brown hair worn in a mountainous pug on top of her head. She was, as everyone said, quick as chain lightning. Fessenden used to boast that she could wait on three customers while he was saying "Good morning" to one.

No one ever got used to the speed with which she figured. She merely put down the prices and, with no perceptible pause, the total beneath them. Travelers, dropping in, always checked her, not believing it could be done, while she stood by, outwardly patient, but inwardly fuming at the time being wasted.

More remarkable still was the way she kept things in her head. When business was heavy, on a Saturday for instance, she did not always write out her charges until the end of the day. Then, sitting by her own kitchen table, while Fessenden talked and argued with the men around the store, she made them out from memory.

J. Clifford	5 lbs. nails @ $.03 lb.	$ .15
	1 halter @ $.15	$ .15
	2 lbs. lard @ $.06½	$ .13
A. Greenleaf	1 barrel corn meal @ $2.80	$2.80
	2 gallons turpentine @ $.30	$ .60
	2 dozen eggs @ $.08	$ .16
L. Holbrook	2 gallons molasses @ $.39	$ .78
	1 lb. rice @ $.06	$ .06
	5 lbs. sugar @ $.05	$ .25
Thomas Orne	1 pr. child's shoes @ $1.12	$1.12
	1 dozen cuff buttons @ $.05	$ .60

She remembered other things. She knew to a day

when you should be running out of molasses, corn meal or pilot bread. "How about kerosene?" she would ask even before she saw you had your can with you. Then while you were opening your pocketbook to see how much money you had, she would dash to the cellar, fill the can and bring it back up with a potato jammed neatly over its spout.

She was as quick, too, in the post office, though she never trusted to her memory here. When the mail came in, she whipped open the grey canvas bag, rolled each paper, flipped each letter in its proper box, and opened the window — all this while a customer was trying on a pair of lumberman's rubbers. She canceled all the letters exactly, with the rapidity and rhythm of a woodpecker.

It was never her fault when the mail was late though she always felt a mortification. She had a variety of drivers to put up with, and their standards were not hers. One — he was on the route for ten years — was a French Canadian named Bob Marie, who could neither read nor write. In winter he wore an enormous bearskin coat tied close at the neck by a grimy pair of underdrawers. No teetotaler, he frequently drank too much, fell out of the sleigh, and lay in the road while the horses plodded on to the post office. Then it was up to Fanny Stone to send a customer to the rescue before someone, seeing only the coat, took a shot at Bob Marie.

She had a quick tongue, too, but one more given to wit than to censure. She always spoke her mind and she usually got away with it. In 1939, when she was guest of James Farley, the postmaster general, at the state convention of postmasters in Augusta, she told him exactly how a fourth-class post office should be run. He listened — and he liked it.

Abundantly healthy, she needed none of the medicines she sold. She handled three jobs — in the store,

in the post office, in the house (she had three children) —
and still had energy left over. Indeed, she seemed to give
it to everyone and everything she touched. Her house
plants — geraniums, begonias, gloxinias — bloomed twice
as profusely and twice as long as anyone else's. One of
her cacti, set out in the front yard every summer, used to
stop passers-by, who tried to count its blossoms but always
gave up. Another, a pond-lily cactus, she kept on the porch
of the store. Nearly everybody in town had a slip from it,
but no slip ever equalled the plant itself. In the garden,
tended when business was slow, were large bleeding
hearts, huge peonies, matchless sweet peas, and a hon-
eysuckle always alive with bees and humming birds.

She vitalized ever organization she joined — the
Wiscasset Woman's Club, the Farm Bureau, the National
League of Postmasters, the Grange. As long as she was a
member no one of them ever got into a rut. No one of
them ever failed in a civic responsibility, either. She did
more than her part. It was she who put across the bond
sales and the Red Cross drives. "Let Fan run it," people
said when a new project came up, knowing that with her
on the job it was as good as done already.

She fought when she had to — and she never lost.
(Any liquor violator was in for her wrath. He didn't last
long in Edgecomb.) Only once did she hold her tongue
against her conscience. That was in 1917 when Women's
Rights became a constitutional issue. Her impulse was to
get out and make speeches in its defense, but since she
was a government employee she felt she could not. So she
had to satisfy herself with privately speaking her mind. It
was her only real frustration.

She was correspondent for the Boothbay *Register*;
anyone reading her columns would have thought that
Edgecomb was the most enterprising town in the State of
Maine. While correspondents from larger areas often began

apologetically, "A quiet week" or "Not very newsy," Fanny Stone plunged right in. She was a born reporter. Nothing missed her eye or ear or pen.

> A large flock of wild geese was seen flying North at 1 P.M. Wednesday. Is it not early for the backbone of winter to be broken?

She recorded every chimney fire, every runaway horse, every new baby.

> Mrs. Staunton Sherman presented her husband with a fine boy (10 lbs) June 11. Mother and babe are doing well. If you listen attentively, you may at any time hear the happy father softly humming a lullaby.

She told who was repairing his roof, who was poorly, who was digging a well, who had relatives visiting on Sunday, who had put in a telephone, who had cut his hay. Unlike other correspondents, she gave complete details.

> Little Rose Emma Trask, while playing Tag this Thursday night, fell and broke the small bone in her left arm. She was attended by Dr. Blake and made comfortable, experiencing little pain, but she lamented greatly to think her fun for the Fourth had been spoiled. Her sister Evelyn fell out of a swing and cut her hand quite badly. We pity the poor little girls being housed this hot weather.

She was a columnist as well as reporter. Nothing printable was too personal for her pen.

> Mrs. Lena Huff has a new hat from the National Suit and Coat Company. It cost $3.

> Mr. Louis P. Hodgdon of Boothbay called on friends Monday. He was en route to Wiscasset, courting.

When she suspected something, she passed her suspicions on.

230

Listen for wedding bells this week. A long happy life to both is the sincere wish of the writer.

When she ran out of news about people, she wrote of other things.

The writer breakfasted one morning this week on lettuce raised by our neighbor, Mrs. J.J. Patterson. Who can beat that for this cold, backward season?

Mr. Freeman Greenleaf had a hen steal her nest away in the haymow and from 26 eggs brought out 21 fine chickens.

Skunks have been playing havoc in George Holman's field. He succeeded in capturing three and a woodchuck this week after they had ruined many hills of early potatoes.

Smart woman that she was, Fanny Stone now and then used her columns to further the business of the store. Advertisements occasionally appeared, always placed between two exciting bits of news where they could not fail to catch the eye.

Have you seen the new post cards with views of Edgecomb? Call at the Post Office and get a set to send to absent friends. They are the best yet.

Call at Stone's store when in need of winter underwear, boots, shoes or rubbers for yourself or children. The "Russet Ranger" a Specialty for men's working shoes. Try a pair.

Fanny Stone knew nothing of the editorial We. Everything she wrote conveyed her own personal warmth and enthusiasm.

Thankful to report that James Philbrick is able to work again. Walks a little lame yet, but can do a good day's work for all of that.

Mr. Ira Holman came from Norwood, Mass. Tuesday to spend several weeks with his nephew, George. He came alone. Pretty smart for an old gentleman past his eightieth year.

O, may the New Year as is comes make life as bright as the blooming rose to all our dear friends and readers of the *Register*.

She was a loyal Baptist though never a literal one. She thought the Bible was a great book — often an exciting one — but she didn't believe its every word, and she found nothing in her reading of it to forbid people to play cards, or to dance either, if they had a mind to. She neither prayed over sinners nor rejoiced at their salvation. But she very zealously kept the Lord's commandments especially as they concerned her neighbor. When other people brought jellies to the house of the sick, Fanny Stone was there already washing sheets. When other people avoided contagion, she was in it. It was Fan Stone who sat up with the dead at night.

But above everything else she was a devoted wife and mother. An earlier marriage, unhappy and never mentioned, had given her a keener appreciation of this one. She didn't care what other people thought about her, she often said, just as long as she suited Fes and the children. And she suited them perfectly.

Instead of feeling sorry for himself, as now and then some Edgecomb woman insisted he ought to, with all Fan's gallivanting, Fes beamed with pride at everything she did. She painted a little with oils, mostly pictures of her garden and of her collie, Prince. Fes was always showing them off in the store. She had dropped her antique mirror and, to cover the crack in the glass, she had painted an artistic spray of flowers over it. "That's Fan," he would say, chuckling, "that's Fan all over."

He liked to have her do things other women didn't dare to do. "Fan's going to get herself a car and drive it," he boasted in 1914 when there was only one other car in town. She did get the car and all during World War I she drove it as a taxi. People from Wiscasset used to call her, knowing she would get there sooner than any local man. Whatever the traveling, she never missed a train.

Fes died in 1932. On the night of his funeral Prince, who had never gone upstairs, led the way to the bedroom and slept on the floor by her bed. "Seemed like he figured it was left to him to be the man," she said. After that he never left her.

With Fes's death Fanny Stone lost some of her zest. But she kept going, taking full responsibility, at the age of seventy, of the post office, the store and the gasoline pump outside. Travelers were often struck by her, and many of those who came in for a cigar or an Eskimo pie, sat for a time on the steps beside the pink cactus. A poet who stopped by on a walking trip put her into stanzas:

> "A queen," we said, "she could have been a queen!
> That fearless heart, that flourishing green
> Bay-tree of spirit, the adept
> Delicate response that kept
> Perfect alignment, the swift word
> Light-footed as a fawn, and as unspurrred."*

*Fantasia on the Sheepscot, Christine Turner Curtis, Bread Loaf Anthology, 1939

Local people — even those who had criticized her — began more and more to appreciate her worth. In 1940 she was the guest of honor at a performance of "What A Life" at the Boothbay Playhouse. Postmaster General Farley, invited to the occasion, sent this letter, which was read that night to a crowded house.

> I congratulate you most heartily upon this recognition. No better choice could be made, for no one can question that The Post Office Department will always be grateful for the fine service you gave prior to your recent retirement as postmaster at Edgecomb. The long period during which you conducted the Post Office was, I know, a source of much satisfaction to the citizens of Edgecomb and to others who had the pleasure of receiving service at your hands.
>
> The play title "What A Life" suggests that when referring to you, we might very well say 'What a Postmaster!'
>
> May I again offer my heartiest congratulations upon this happy occasion, and extend to you and the cast of "What A Life" my very best wishes.

She died three years later, in January 1943, from pneumonia following a fractured hip. It was her first real illness; in all her forty-seven years of government service, she had missed only fifteen days.

People from all over the county turned out for her funeral. At its close, someone was heard to say, "Seems like it's the town that's dead now, instead of Fan."

Sources of Material
for Part Two

SAMUEL TRASK: The Essex Institute, Salem, Mass.; New England Historic and Genealogical Register; records of the Town of Edgecomb.

MOSES DAVIS: Diary of Moses Davis; records of the Town of Edgecomb.

STEPHEN PARSONS: Maine Historical Society, Portland, Maine; New England Historical and Genealogical Register; records of the Town of Edgecomb.

MUTINY: Local historians Fanny Chase and George Chase; Emma Patterson Diary (Fanny Chase papers); Maine Historical Society, Portland.

VILLAGE SCHOOL: School books loaned by local residents, especially the Greenleaf and Cunningham families; reminiscences of George Chase.

VILLAGE LIBRARY: Books loaned by local residents, especially by the Cunningham family; records of the Town of Edgecomb.

VILLAGE POSTMASTER: Local residents and contemporary newspapers; Boothbay Harbor Public Library and Boothbay *Register*.

LOYALIST: New England Historical and Genealogical Register; Journal of Jacob Bailey, Massachusetts Historical Society, Boston; Fanny Chase papers.

SHIPWRECK: Reference Room, Boston Public Library. See text.